Phone Numbers

School name, phone: _____

Teacher's name, phone: _____

School counselor's name, phone: _____

School name, phone: _____

Teacher's name, phone: _____

School counselor's name, phone: _____

Coach's name, phone: _____

Coach's name, phone: _____

Clubs or groups for teens:
Name: _____ Phone: _____

Name: _____ Phone: _____

Name: _____ Phone: _____

Name: _____ Phone: _____

Teen's friends:
Name: _____ Phone: _____

Name: _____ Phone: _____

Name: _____ Phone: _____

Name: _____ Phone: _____

Other phone numbers:
Name: _____ Phone: _____

Name: _____ Phone: _____

Name: _____ Phone: _____

Name: _____ Phone: _____

What To Do
For Your Teen's Health

Easy to Read • Easy to Use

Gloria Mayer, R.N.
Ann Kuklierus, R.N.

Institute for Healthcare Advancement
501 S. Idaho St., Suite 300
La Habra, California 90631
(800) 434-4633

© 2013 by Institute for Healthcare Advancement
501 S. Idaho St., Suite 300
La Habra, California 90631
(800) 434-4633

Printed in the United States of America
16 15 14 13 10 9 8 7 6 5 4 3 2 1
ISBN: 978-0-9720148-9-2

To Our Readers

This book is for moms, dads, and others who have teens. It explains the body changes that happen to teens. It will help you explain these changes to your teen.

This book gives you tips on how to deal with teen issues. These include dating, school, bullying, driving, smoking, and drugs. It will help you talk with your teen about these things.

This book tells you about the signs of trouble and where to get help. It will help you understand the teen years. This can help you keep your teen safe and healthy.

Here are some things to do when you get this book.

- Fill in the phone numbers in the front of the book. Keep this book where it is easy to find.
- Turn to page 5 to see what's in this book.
- See page 3 to learn when you should get help for your teen. Read pages 41–43, "Getting Help for Your Teen," for a list of people and places to get help for your teen.
- Read a few pages of this book every day until you have read it all.
- See the word list on page 172. It tells you what some words in the book mean.

To Our Readers

This book was written by nurses and read by doctors and others who work with teens. They agree with what's in this book. They feel it is safe and helpful advice.

But each teen is different. Some things in this book may not be right for your teen. You must decide what to do and when to get help. If you are worried about your teen or have questions, get help right away.

There are many people you can go to for help, such as:

- Doctors and nurses
- School teachers and counselors
- Social workers
- Therapists
- Priests, ministers, rabbis, or other religious leaders
- Hotlines and support groups

Always do what your doctor or other trained persons tell you.

When to Get Help Right Away

Your teen is changing. It is hard to know what is normal and what is not. **Get help if your teen does any of these things:**

- Talks about dying, hurting himself or herself, or taking his or her own life
- Is giving things away
- Is mean to animals
- Takes drugs or gets drunk
- Fights a lot
- Threatens to run away
- Has no friends, or spends too much time alone
- Comes and goes without talking to anyone in the family
- Has had unprotected sex or may be pregnant

Get help if any of these things happen to your teen:

- Is raped
- Loses or gains a lot of weight
- Looks sick or is always tired
- Seems angry all the time
- Is failing in school
- Gets into trouble with the law

Read this book for more signs of when to get help for your teen.

When to Get Help Right Away

Here are some places that you can call to get help. Some are open 24 hours a day, 7 days a week.

National Parent Helpline	1-855-427-2736
Boys Town National Family Hotline	1-800-448-3000
Partnership for Drug-Free America Parents Helpline	1-855-378-4373
National Council on Alcoholism and Drug Dependence	1-800-622-2255
Substance Abuse and Mental Health Services	1-800-662-4357
American Lung Association (Quit Smoking)	1-800-586-4872
National Eating Disorder Association Helpline	1-800-931-2237
National Runaway Safeline	1-800-786-2929
National Center for Missing and Exploited Children Call Center	1-800-843-5678
Childhelp National Child Abuse Hotline	1-800-422-4453
National Domestic Violence Hotline	1-800-799-7233
National Sexual Assault Hotline (RAINN)	1-800-656-4673
National Teen Dating Abuse Helpline (Love Is Respect)	1-866-331-9474
Abstinence Clearinghouse	1-888-577-2966
AIDS Info	1-800-448-0440
CDC AIDS and Sexually Transmitted Disease (STD) Info Hotline	1-800-232-4636
Planned Parenthood STD, Birth Control and Pregnancy Hotline	1-800-230-7526
America's Pregnancy Helpline	1-800-672-2296
Birthright Pregnancy Helpline	1-800-550-4900
Gay Lesbian Bisexual Transgender (GLBT) National Hotline	1-800-843-4564
The Trevor Project GLBT Lifeline	1-866-488-7386
National Suicide Prevention Lifeline	1-800-273-8255
National Hopeline Suicide Prevention Network	1-800-442-4673

What's in This Book

The Teen Years:
A Time of Big Changes

1

Notes

_____

_____

_____

_____

_____

_____

_____

_____

_____

_____

_____

_____

_____

_____

Emotions

What is it?

Emotions are very strong feelings. A teen's emotions can change very fast. Teens may be happy one minute and sad the next.

Did you know?

As children become teens, their needs change. Your role as a parent also changes. This is normal.

Teens can cry, laugh, or get angry all in a short time. This is called mood swings. Mood swings are normal. They come from changes in the hormones of growing boys and girls.

Mood swings also come from pressure that a teen may feel. Pressure comes from the many changes that happen:

- Body changes
- More duties at home
- Harder schoolwork
- Friends are changing

Teens need to learn how to deal with pressure. Parents can teach teens how to relax and deal with pressure. They can help teens learn how to manage their feelings.

Teens often don't know what they feel or want. They don't know why they are sad. Ask how your teen feels. Talk with your teen about these feelings. This can help your teen learn what is right and wrong.

Teens may say they love and hate their parents. This is normal. Teens want to be left alone. At the same time, they want help from their parents.

Teens worry about many things:

- School grades
- Money
- Not having enough time
- What other people think of them
- Friends
- Their future

Teens may not seem to care about things, but they care very much.

What can I do?

Tell your teen that body changes affect how a person feels. Say that this is normal.

Spend time with your teen. Find out how your teen is feeling. Ask what your teen worries about. Listen to what your teen says, even if you don't agree. When your teen talks, don't say it's right or wrong. Just let your teen talk about things.

Praise your teen for doing things right. Accept your teen. Never make fun of your teen. Don't tease your teen.

Teens often copy what others do. Set a good example for how you want your teen to act.

Talk with your teen about feelings. Watch for signs of anger. Anger is a strong feeling. It can be a problem. If you don't help your teen with anger, bad things may happen. (Read about Anger on page 74.)

Tell your whole family not to fight with your teen. If your teen acts badly, give your teen space and time to cool off.

Know what your teen does every day. Meet your teen's friends.

When you punish your teen, try to be fair. Don't over-punish your teen for something small. Pick your fights. Don't fight over small things.

Set limits for your teen. Also talk about important things your teen needs to do. When you can, let your teen decide things. Even if you don't like what your teen wears, it may be OK to wear it. This lets teens have their way about safe things.

Try to include your teen in family time, but don't force it.

Be honest with your teen. Respect your teen. Listen carefully. Don't accuse your teen of anything without having all the facts.

Don't lecture to your teen. Discuss things with your teen.

Teach your teen how to deal with pressure. Talk to your teen. Show your teen how to relax. Help your teen learn to plan and arrange things.

When should I get help?

- Your teen has no friends. Your teen spends too much time alone.
- Your teen is angry or sad most of the time.
- You and your teen fight all the time. You can't talk with your teen.
- Your teen is getting into trouble at school.
- You are afraid your teen will get into trouble with the law.

Body Changes in Boys

What is it?

A boy's body changes from a child to an adult during the teen years. This time of fast growth is called puberty. With these body changes, a boy can get a girl pregnant.

Did you know?

Changes can start in boys anytime from 8–15 years old. Changes take 3–5 years.

These are the changes that happen:

- Fine, straight hairs start to grow around the penis. These hairs get dark and thick.
- The balls (testicles) grow bigger. So does the sac they are in (scrotum).
- The penis grows wider and longer.
- The boy's voice starts to change and get deeper.
- Hairs start to grow on his upper lip.
- Hair grows under his arms and on his face.
- The boy grows taller.

Here are pictures showing how a boy's body changes.

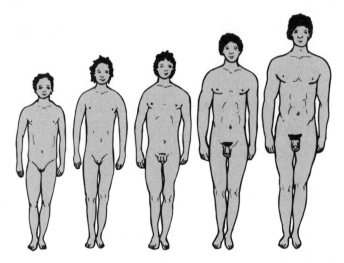

Boys grow tall in the later teen years. A boy is tall like an adult by age 18. Boys who eat healthy and exercise get strong and look lean.

A boy's voice gets deeper during this time. His voice may crack when he talks. This is normal.

A boy's penis starts to shoot out (ejaculate) a liquid called semen. When this happens during the night it is called a wet dream. There is nothing a boy can do to stop wet dreams. They are normal. Wet dreams happen less often after a boy's body changes end.

A boy can get a girl pregnant once he has semen. This happens between 11 and 17 years old.

A boy's penis may get hard at any time. This is called an erection. Erections can happen without touching the penis or thinking of sex. This is normal.

Some boys' breasts get bigger. They may feel a bump under one or both nipples. This is normal and will go away.

Balls (testicles) may not be the same size. This is normal.

Some boys get circumcised when they are babies. A doctor cuts off the extra skin over the tip of the penis. This is called the foreskin. The penis looks different if the foreskin is gone. Both ways are normal.

circumcised   uncircumcised

A boy's body starts to smell at this time. Boys need to take a shower every day. They need to use deodorant under their arms.

What can I do?

Talk with your teen about body changes before they start. Tell your teen the changes are normal. Don't make fun of your teen's body changes. Teens worry about what people say about their bodies.

Show your teen the pictures in this book. Let him ask questions. Explain wet dreams and erections. Tell him that it may make him blush or feel shy. Give him ideas on how to hide an erection, like wearing big shirts and pants.

Talk about washing the penis. If he has a foreskin, tell him to pull it back when washing.

Talk about body smell and the need to shower and use deodorant.

By this time, your teen needs to know how babies are made.

When should I get help?

* Your teen has pain in his groin or sex parts.
* Your teen can't pull back the foreskin to wash his penis.
* He is having sex.
* He has pain when he pees.
* He is a lot shorter than his friends.
* Pus is coming out of his penis.
* You don't know how to talk with your teen about sex.

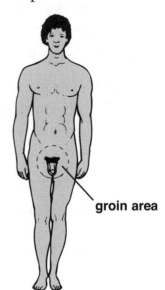

groin area

Body Changes in Girls

What is it?

A girl's body changes from a child to an adult during the teen years. This time of fast growth is called puberty. These changes let girls have babies.

Did you know?

Changes can start in girls anytime from ages 8–14. Changes can last for 4–5 years.

These are the body changes that happen:

- Hairs start to grow around the vagina. The hair there gets dark and curly.
- Breasts begin to grow. At first they look like little bumps under the nipples. Then they grow to their full size and shape.
- The red area around the nipples grows out from the chest.
- The girl grows taller.
- Hair grows on her legs, under her arms, and around the genitals.
- The girl starts her period. This is called menstruation.

Here are pictures showing how a girl's body changes.

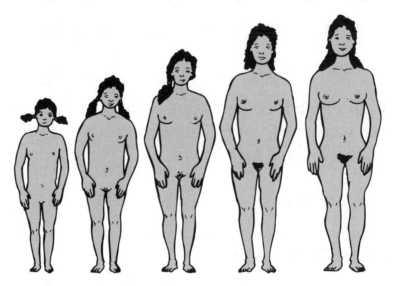

Girls grow tall during the early teen years. They stop growing at around age 16. Girls gain weight during this time. They need to gain some weight to start having their period. This does not mean that girls get fat.

Periods can start between ages 10 and 14. Most girls get their period around 12–13 years old. Fluid leaks from the vagina before the period starts. The fluid can be clear or white. It can be watery or thick. This is normal.

At first, her period is not regular. She can skip a month. A period lasts from 2–5 days. At first a girl may have no pain with a period. Later she may have cramps the first few days. Motrin or other over-the-counter pain medicines can help the pain.

One breast may grow bigger than the other. The small one will catch up. The breasts may be sore while they are growing. This is normal.

A girl's body starts to smell at this time. Girls need to shower every day. They need to use deodorant under their arms.

Girls worry about their bodies. They wonder if these changes are normal.

What can I do?

Talk with your teen about body changes before the changes start. Talk about breast and hair growth, periods, and normal vaginal fluid. Tell her the changes are normal. Don't make fun of your teen's body changes. Girls worry about what people say about their bodies.

Teach her what to do when she gets her period. This is very important. She needs to know this before she has her first period. Show her things she will need for her period, like pads and tampons. Make sure she can get them at school. She may also carry them with her.

Do something nice with your teen when she gets her first period. Don't say bad things about her period or breast growth. Don't call her period a "curse" or use other bad names.

Talk with your teen about body smells and what to do. Your teen will need to shower every day and use deodorant.

Your teen should know how babies are made before her first period. Tell your teen about how the egg drops into the uterus so she can get pregnant. This is called ovulation.

Listen to your teen's feelings about growing up. She may fear leaving her childhood behind.

When should I get help?

- Your teen has not had a period by age 14.
- She has a lot of pain with her period. The pain does not go away after taking Motrin or other over-the-counter pain medicines.
- Your teen is having sex.
- She is much shorter than her friends.
- Your teen has fluid coming from her vagina that does not look normal.
- You don't know how to teach her what to do for her period.
- You don't know how to talk with your teen about sex.

How Parents Can Help Teens

2

Notes

_____

_____

_____

_____

_____

_____

_____

_____

_____

_____

_____

_____

_____

Body Image and Self-Esteem

What is it?

Body image and self-esteem are how teens feel about the way they look.

Did you know?

Body changes may make teens feel insecure. Teens worry about how they look. They may feel too short or too fat. They may worry about pimples (acne). They may feel their hair is too thin or frizzy. Teens need help to accept their bodies. They need help to be happy with how they look.

The teen years are hard on self-esteem. Parents and friends help shape how teens see themselves. Saying nice things to teens makes them feel good. Teens feel good when they do well in school, sports, and other things, too. This builds up self-esteem.

Teens with high self-esteem make good choices. Teens with low self-esteem are not happy. They feel they are not good enough.

Low self-esteem is bad for a teen's health.

Teens with low self-esteem don't take good care of their bodies.

They may do any of these things that are harmful:

- Smoke
- Drink alcohol
- Take drugs
- Cut themselves
- Bully others
- Eat too much or too little

Teens need to build a strong and healthy body. Teens need to learn to be happy with who they are. It is normal for teens to think about how their bodies look. It is normal for teens to think about who they are. Teens who don't accept who they are may have health problems later in life.

Acne is a problem for many teens. Acne can mean blackheads or whiteheads, bumps, pimples with pus, or bright red skin. A teen's face can swell and be sore to touch. Teens with acne may feel shy and try to hide their faces. Acne can cause pain and scars.

What can I do?

Teens need to feel good about who they are and how they look. Here are some things you can do to help:

- Praise your teen often, but be honest.
- Brag about your teen. Let your teen hear you.

- Help your teen find things your teen is good at. Your teen may like music, sports, or art.

- Tell your teen often, "I'm proud of you." This will help your teen's self-esteem.

Help your teen have a healthy body. Serve healthy meals. Get your teen to exercise 1 hour every day and sleep 8–9 hours each night.

Don't call your teen names like "stupid." Don't put your teen down.

Don't pick on small things. Don't look for reasons to correct your teen. Look for reasons to praise your teen. Praise your teen's successes. Give your teen a special present if a school test goes well.

Teens need to hear their parents say they love them. And they need to hear it often. Put notes in your teen's bag or other places where your teen will find them. Here are some things you can write:

- I'm thinking about you.
- You can do it!
- You are terrific!
- You are special!
- Good luck on your test.
- I'm proud of you.
- Here's a hug. Have a great day!

Talk to your teen about what makes a good friend. (Read about Friends on page 47.)

Help your teen as soon as you see acne. Here are some tips for you and your teen:

- Teens should wash their face with a mild soap 2 times a day. Tell your teen not to scrub. Tell your teen not to touch the face between washings.

- These things make acne worse: oily makeup, picking or squeezing pimples, and stress. Tight collars, headbands, and other things against the skin can make acne worse, too.

- Go to a drugstore and talk to the pharmacist. Ask about a cream or ointment that your teen can use for acne. Find out how to use it the right way. Don't use too much at one time.

- Go to a doctor with your teen if the acne is bad.

When should I get help?

- Your teen always says bad things about himself or herself.
- Your teen will not try new things.
- Your teen is always afraid of failing.
- Your teen spends most of the time alone.
- You are worried about your teen.
- Your teen has lost interest in favorite hobbies or sports.
- Your teen has acne that does not get better.

Family Time

What is it?

Family time is when
everyone in the family does
something together. Family
can be a mom, dad, and
kids. It can be grandparents,
a single mom, single dad, step-parents, or others.

Did you know?

Teens who are close to their families have fewer problems
with drugs and the law. Being with family teaches teens
values. It teaches them how to get along with others.

The teen years can be full of hard times. Teens need family
when they are sad or worried.

Teens may act like they don't want to be part of the family.
They may think it's not cool to be seen with their parents.
Teens often feel like little kids when they are with their
parents. So they may set rules:

- No hugs or kisses in public.
- They want to be dropped off at the corner.
- They don't want to be seen with their parents.

Teens love their parents. They just don't show it. Being with
friends and doing outside things seem more important than
family. This is normal. Parents must slowly let go of teens.
Letting go can be hard for parents.

What can I do?

Spend time with your teen. Look for ways to stay close to your teen. Do things alone with your teen, like shopping or having lunch.

Teens need to feel part of a group. Make the family your teen's group.

Set aside one night a week as family night. Do something together as a family on that night. If your family goes to church or temple, do it together.

Do things as a family, such as camping or hiking. Start a family project, like planting a garden. Take up a family sport.

Eat several meals a week as a family. It can be hard to get everyone together, but it is important. It is a good time to stay in touch with your teen. Turn off the TV, music, and cell phones. It's a time for the family to talk and laugh together. Have your teen help with planning and cooking the meal, and cleaning up, too.

Plan things to do as a family. Your teen may not want to join in. If that happens, ask if your teen would like to bring a friend along.

Give your teen some power in the family. Let your teen make choices sometimes. This will make your teen feel good. Let your teen choose:

- Where to go out to eat
- What to have for dinner
- Which movie to see

Kids in a family often fight. It is best to let them work things out on their own. Don't take sides. Set rules, such as no hitting.

Don't let your teen have a TV or computer in the bedroom. Your teen will spend too much time alone. Keep the TV and computer in the family area. This will help your teen spend more time with the family. You will also be able to see what your teen is watching and doing.

Give your teen jobs to do as part of the family. Some things your teen can do:

- Wash the family car
- Take out the trash
- Wash the dishes
- Keep a neat bedroom

When should I get help?

- Your teen is never at home.
- Your teen refuses to be part of the family.
- Your teen feels like a stranger to you.
- You can't talk with your teen.

Love and Understanding

What is it?

It is seeing good things in your teen all the time.

Did you know?

Teens need their parents to love and understand them. They need to feel hope. They need to know:

- The teen years will pass.
- Everything will be OK.
- One day they will be happy adults.
- They will have a good future.

Teens who get love and understanding at home are less likely to break the law. They don't need to find love and support in gangs.

What can I do?

Read about the changes that happen to teens (see pages 7–20). This will help you understand why teens act the way they do.

Love and accept your teen. Look for the good in your teen all the time. The teen years will pass. It may feel like forever right now. Soon your teen will grow up and move away.

You can build a strong bond for the future by loving and understanding your teen today.

Talk with your teen about how hard the teen years are. Tell your teen about problems and fears you had when you were a teen. This will show you understand.

Before you get upset, ask yourself: "How big a deal is this?" Don't get upset over small things, like if your teen didn't put out the trash.

Your teen will make mistakes. Learn to overlook some things. Don't pick on your teen for everything.

Say nice things to your teen. Talk about things your teen does that you like. Talk about what your teen does well.

When should I get help?

- You are having a hard time talking with your teen.
- Your teen will not let you get close.
- You don't feel love for your teen.
- You and your teen always fight.

Rules and Discipline

What is it?

Rules are limits put on teens' actions. Rules are also things teens need to do. Discipline is something you do as a parent. It is when adults correct teens if they break a rule or do something wrong.

Did you know?

Teens need some rules or limits. It helps teens feel safe. It helps them know what is right.

Parents set rules for things such as:

- What time to come home at night (curfew)
- Dating
- How much TV to watch
- Homework
- Driving
- No smoking, alcohol, or drugs
- Chores at home
- Telling the truth

Teens should not have too many rules. The rules should be fair. The rules need to be the same when parents are in a good mood or a bad mood. This makes teens feel secure. They know how to act and what to expect.

Rules and Discipline

Teens need to know what will happen if they break the rules. Teens like to test the rules. This is normal. When you discipline a teen fairly, you help the teen learn what is right. You also help keep the teen safe.

Here are the most common ways to discipline teens:

- Take away things like using the phone, TV, or car.
- Don't allow a teen to go out. This is called grounding.
- Take away a teen's allowance.

It's not good to discipline too harshly. Try to be fair. For example, if your teen comes home 30 minutes late from a date, it may be unfair to ground the teen for a month.

Disciplining teens the same way you do young children doesn't work. Sending teens to their rooms won't teach them anything. That's where a teen wants to be.

What can I do?

Set family rules. Tell your teen what you expect.

Set clear rules. Say, "Be home by 10 p.m." Don't say, "Be home early." This is not clear.

Don't make too many rules. Teens need to start making their own choices.

Be fair. Think before you act. Don't discipline your teen when you are angry. You may be too harsh. Next time your teen breaks a rule, ask what your teen thinks you should do. Your teen may surprise you.

Rules and Discipline

Your teen is watching and learning from you. Make sure your teen learns the right things. Don't look for reasons to correct your teen. Look for reasons to praise your teen. Think back on what you said to your teen today. Did you say any nice things?

Discipline your teen out of love, not anger. Your teen will make you very angry at times. Stay calm. Don't lose your cool! Take deep breaths before you speak or act.

Never hit your teen. This could start a pattern of violence. Control yourself, no matter how angry you are. Walk away if you think you may lose control.

If you lose control, tell your teen you are sorry. You made a mistake. Your teen will respect you. It will teach your teen what to do when your teen makes a mistake.

Make sure your teen feels loved, even when your teen does something wrong. Tell your teen you are upset with what happened. Make it clear that you still love your teen. Hug your teen every day.

Make sure your teen knows you are always there to help. When your teen comes to you, don't yell or get angry. Stay calm. Teach by your example how to listen and fix a problem.

Don't try to fix everything. Let your teen solve some problems alone. Help your teen learn from mistakes. Help your teen learn by asking these questions:

- What did you learn?
- What can you do to make things right?
- What can you do so you don't make the same mistake again?

Rules and Discipline

Teach your teen that there are small mistakes and big mistakes in life. We can fix small mistakes such as:

- Failing a test
- Coming home late
- Missing sports practice

Big mistakes hurt and limit a teen's life forever. Some big mistakes are:

- Breaking the law
- Using drugs
- Getting pregnant

Teach your teen to think before doing something that could be a big mistake.

Don't be too hard on your teen over a small mistake. Your teen may get angry and fight back. Or, your teen may be afraid to come to you next time.

Don't try to control your teen's every move. This may make your teen angry. Teens need to make some choices and mistakes. This helps with learning. Your actions should show that you trust and respect your teen. Don't forget to praise your teen for following the rules. Say things like:

- "I noticed you came home on time last night. I'm proud of you."
- "You did a good job cleaning your room. It looks very nice."

When should I get help?

- Your teen is getting into trouble with the law.
- Your teen refuses to follow the family rules.
- You can't control your anger or your temper.
- You are hitting your teen.
- Your teen is hitting you.
- Your teen lies all the time.
- Your teen is using drugs.

Talking With Your Teen

What is it?

Talking with your teen shows love. Talking is the way to stay close to your teen. It's how you learn about your teen's feelings, fears, and dreams.

Did you know?

It's very important for parents to talk with their teen. Talking can be hard. It may end in yelling. Teens react to:

- Words
- Tone of voice
- The look on the parent's face

What can I do?

Use any free time to talk with your teen. A good time to talk is when you and your teen are in the car.

Talk with your teen the way you would like your teen to talk with you. Try these things:

- Stop what you are doing. Listen to your teen. Your teen will listen better if you listen first.

- Ask questions to make sure you understand.
- Keep your voice normal.
- Don't lecture your teen.
- Don't tease or make fun of your teen.
- Be patient with your teen.

Say you are sorry if you make a mistake.

Always try to answer your teen's questions. Tell your teen if you don't know the answer. Then, find the answer together.

Here are two examples of a parent and teen talking. Note how the teen reacts to what the parent says.

The wrong way to talk with your teen:

Teen: See you later.

Parent: Just where do you think you're going?

Teen: Out!

Parent: No, you're not! You know the rules. Since you failed your math test, you're not going out all week.

Teen: But I'm going to Tom's house to work on math.

Parent: No way. He dropped out of school. He's a bum who does nothing all day. He's trying to get you into trouble.

Teen: That's not true! You just don't like him.

Parent: What's there to like? Just look at him: shaved head, ring in the nose, tattoos. He's a bum!

Teen: You don't like any of my friends! Sometimes I wonder if you like me!

Parent: That's enough stupid talk. Go to your room and do your homework!

Teen: You can't tell me what to do! I'm going out.

Parent: If you walk out that door, don't bother coming back!

Teen: Fine, I'll just stay at Tom's!

A better way to talk with your teen:

Teen: See you later.

Parent: It's a school night. Where are you going?

Teen: I'm going to Tom's to study.

Parent: Is there something I can help you with?

Teen: No, I just need a break.

Parent: You have been working hard, and I'm proud of you. But remember what we agreed to? You are not supposed to go out until you catch up on your homework.

Teen: I know, but I need a break.

Parent: Then why don't we go for a walk around the block together?

Teen: No thanks. I think I'll just go back to my room.

When should I get help?

- Your teen refuses to talk with you.
- You and your teen can't talk without yelling.
- You are worried about your teen.

Getting Help for Your Teen

What is it?

How to find help for your teen and you.

Did you know?

The teen years can be hard on everyone in the family.

Your teen is changing. You may not know when to give your teen more freedom. You may not be able to stop your teen from doing something wrong.

There are times when you need an answer to a question. Sometimes you need to talk with someone. There are times when you are not sure what to do. There may be times when you have an emergency.

Some problems are too big for parents to handle alone. Here are some ways to find help:

- Talk to other parents about where they found help.

- Ask your health insurance company where to go for help.

- Look for groups near where you live. Places like the YMCA, Boys and Girls Club, and Planned Parenthood can help you.

- Check with your County or State's Health Department to see if they can help you.
- Listen to TV or radio ads for classes and programs.
- Check if your work has an Employee Assistance Program (EAP).
- Ask around for programs on smoking and using drugs or alcohol. Ask about programs your teen can attend. Some programs include AA – Alcoholics Anonymous and NA – Narcotics Anonymous.
- Go to a health clinic or Family Resource Center and ask for help.
- Go to your place of worship and ask for help.
- Go to a cultural center to ask for help.
- Go to the public library. Look for booklets about services. Ask the person at the counter about help in your community.
- Go to the school's main office. Ask who you can talk to about problems your teen is having at school. Ask where you should go for help.
- See your doctor. Ask for a referral to get help. Talk to the staff in the office. Look for booklets and lists of programs that might help.

There are places that you can call to get help. Some are open 24 hours a day, 7 days a week. (See the list of places to call on page 4.)

What can I do?

It is better to get help early. Get help as soon as you think there is a problem.

- Don't wait until your teen is in trouble with the law.
- Don't wait until your teen has a bad habit, like smoking, drinking, or taking drugs.
- Don't wait until your teen drops out of school.

Take a class. Talk to a counselor. Get help. Go alone to get help if your teen won't go with you. When asking for help do not give up easily. Ask again. Let people know you really want help.

Don't wait to get help. You are doing the right thing by asking for help. It could save your teen's life.

When should I get help?

- Call 911 when you or your teen is in danger.
- Get help when you do not know what to do.
- See page 3 for when to get help right away.

Teen Issues

3

Notes

_____

_____

_____

_____

_____

_____

_____

_____

_____

_____

_____

_____

_____

_____

_____

_____

Friends

What is it?

Friends are teens who like each other. They spend a lot of time together. They have things in common and like the same things.

Did you know?

Friends around the same age are called peers. Teens need friends. Friends help teens learn and grow.

A teen's friends can be more important than family. Teens often want to spend more time with friends than with family.

There are two kinds of friends: "good" friends and "bad" friends. Good friends help teens to be their best. They help teens build high self-esteem. Bad friends make teens do things that are wrong.

Teens want to fit in with their friends. That is why it is important for teens to choose the right friends. Teens want to:

- Dress the way their friends dress
- Eat what their friends eat
- Act the way their friends act
- Do what their friends do

Girls often have one best friend. They spend hours talking. They share their feelings. Boys often hang out with several friends. They do things together.

Teens often do what their friends tell them. This is called peer pressure. Teens don't want to be different. They don't want to lose their friends. Peer pressure can make teens do good things like:

- Study and get good grades
- Join a club
- Play sports
- Get a part-time job

Peer pressure can be bad. It can make teens do bad things like:

- Drink and drive
- Drop out of school
- Have sex before the teen is ready
- Lie and steal
- Take drugs

Teens who are close to their families don't give in as often to bad peer pressure. (Read about Family Time on page 27.)

What can I do?

Talk with your teen every day. Be part of your teen's life. Show that you care. Know what your teen is doing. Help your teen find good friends.

Some good places for teens are:

- The YMCA
- School clubs
- Volunteer groups
- Study groups
- Girl Scouts/Boy Scouts
- Church groups
- Community centers
- Sports teams

Get to know your teen's friends. Invite them to your home. Get to know the parents of your teen's friends.

Be friendly with your teen's "good" friends. Invite them to do things with your family.

You can't pick your teen's friends. You can help by pointing out to your teen things you see.

Don't judge your teen's friends by how they look. Talk to your teen at an early age about friends. Teach your teen that good friends are those who:

- Support you
- Care about you
- Respect you
- Are fun to be with
- Make you feel good about yourself

Teach your teen that bad friends are those who:
- Say bad things about you to others
- Try to control you
- Put you down
- Get mad at you all the time
- Pressure you to do things
- Hurt your feelings
- Make you feel that you are not good enough

Talk with your teen about peer pressure. Practice with your teen what to say or do when friends want to do something wrong. This is called role-playing. You can play the friend.

It hurts to lose a friend. Comfort your teen if this happens.

Your teen may want to spend too much time with friends. Find ways to stay close to your teen (see Family Time on page 27).

When should I get help?
- Your teen does not have any friends.
- Your teen is very shy.
- You think your teen is with the wrong friends.
- You are not allowed to meet your teen's friends.

School

What is it?

School prepares teens for life. It teaches them the skills they need.

Did you know?

Teens do better in school if their parents are involved. Some teens do poorly in school. Here are some reasons:

- Some teens don't know how to study. They don't know how to take notes in class. They don't know how to use the library.

- Some teens don't want to work hard. They don't like to do homework. They don't try.

- Some teens have problems learning. This is called a learning disorder. Other teens have a hard time learning because of problems in their home.

Learning disorders often run in families. A learning disorder is not your teen's fault. Teens with a learning disorder can still learn. But they need help. Here are some signs of a learning disorder:

- Mixes up letters or numbers. May write 89 instead of 98 or "left" instead of "felt"

- Has a hard time reading out loud

- Has trouble writing papers
- Has handwriting that is hard to read
- Has trouble remembering facts

Homework can be hard for teens. Some teens stay up late doing homework. They feel a lot of stress. Some parents put too much pressure on teens to do well in school. Teens can get stressed and depressed. They can have other problems, too.

What can I do?

Show your teen that you care about learning. Ask your teen about school every day. Talk to your teen about what is being taught at school. This shows that you care.

Show your teen that school is important. Be part of your teen's school. Go to open houses and all school meetings. Meet your teen's teachers. Do this even if your teen is doing well at school.

Reading gets easier the more you do it. Good reading skills make school easier. Read books in front of your teen. Teach your teen to read for fun.

Know the rules at your teen's school. Talk with your teen about the rules. For example, what happens if a teen is caught smoking? What about drugs? What if a teen brings a knife to school?

Know how your teen is doing in school. Look over your teen's schoolwork. Ask questions. Praise your teen.

If your teen is not doing well at school, find out why. Meet with your teen's teachers.

There are many reasons your teen may not be doing well:

- Your teen may need help with planning.

- Your teen may be too busy.

- Your teen may have a learning disorder.

- Your teen may need some extra help with schoolwork.

Watch for signs that your teen studies all the time. Help your teen balance schoolwork and fun. Don't make your teen study things you like. Support what your teen likes. Help your teen find things your teen is good at.

Don't compare your teen to friends or others in the family who are doing better. This will hurt your teen's self-esteem. Your teen will feel put down. Your teen may stop trying at school.

Don't put too much pressure on your teen. Not all teens can get straight A's. If your teen is working hard and gets B's or C's, that's OK.

Don't get angry if your teen fails a test or class. Stay calm. Try to find out why your teen failed. Never say things like "You're stupid" or "You're lazy." This will hurt your teen's feelings and self-esteem.

Praise your teen's hard work and effort. Say things like, "I can see you worked hard on this paper. I'm proud of you." This kind of praise helps teens feel good about who they are.

Special teachers can help your teen. They are called tutors. Get a tutor if your teen is getting poor grades.

Don't do your teen's homework. Teens must do their own homework. Here are some ways you can help:

- Make sure your teen has a quiet, well-lit place to do homework.
- Talk to your teen about school projects. Help your teen come up with good ideas.
- Set limits on TV time and video games.
- Sit nearby and read a book.
- Bring your teen a snack.
- Make sure your teen gets enough rest.

Watch for signs that your teen is having problems at school. Some things are:

- Your teen does not want to go to school.
- Your teen is often sick and misses school.

- Your teen feels disliked by a teacher.
- Your teen is caught cheating.

Get to know your teen's teachers and school counselor. Talk with them about how your teen is doing.

If you have a computer at home, keep it in the family area. Watch what your teen does on the computer. (Read about rules for using the Internet on page 82.)

When should I get help?

- Your teen fails a class.
- Your teen's grades drop.
- Your teen is getting into trouble at school.
- You are worried about your teen.
- You and your teen always fight about homework.
- Your teen wants to drop out of school.
- Your teen stops going to school.
- Your teen has signs of a learning disorder (see page 51).

Exercise

What is it?

Body movement that makes the heart and breathing go faster.

Did you know?

Regular exercise builds strong bodies. Exercise is also good for other reasons:

- Helps with stress
- Can be fun
- Helps control hunger and weight
- Can help you feel better
- Helps you think more clearly

Many teens don't get enough exercise. They watch too much TV. Some teens watch 20–25 hours of TV a week. Teens also spend a lot of time on the phone, on the Internet, or playing video games.

There are many things a teen can do for exercise, such as:

- Bike riding
- Dancing
- Jogging
- Walking the dog

- Swimming
- Sports

Some teens exercise too much and become too thin. This is a sign of other problems (see Anorexia, page 64). Girls can stop having their period from too much exercise. Teens can get hurt from exercising the wrong way.

What can I do?

A teen needs to exercise at least 60 minutes each day. Three days each week should include exercises to strengthen muscles, like push-ups. Three days each week should include activities to strengthen bones, like jump rope or running.

Help your teen to be active. Limit time watching TV, playing video games, and sitting around.

Help your teen set exercise goals. Praise your teen for being active. If your teen exercises and looks better, say so.

Exercise with your teen. Go on runs or walks together. It's a good time to talk with your teen. It's a good way to get rid of stress.

Help your teen be safe during exercise. Make sure your teen wears the right shoes.

Teens need to wear a helmet for biking, skateboarding, riding scooters, and other sports.

Watch for signs that your teen works out too much. Some signs are losing weight and sore muscles. Teach your teen what to do when there is pain or a muscle is pulled. Use the word RICE to remember what to do:

- **R**est the area that hurts.
- **I**ce the area for 30 minutes every 4 hours for 24 hours.
- **C**ompress or wrap the area.
- **E**levate (raise) the hurt area higher than the heart.

Teens learn by example. Get the whole family to exercise. Go for a fast walk in the evening. Go biking on weekends. Exercise is a good way for the family to spend time together.

When should I get help?

- Your teen refuses to be active and is putting on weight.
- Your teen exercises too much and is losing too much weight.
- Your teen has pain or swelling that does not get better with care at home.

Sports

What is it?

Sports are different games with rules. You move around a lot and get exercise when you play.

Did you know?

Sports are good for teens for many reasons:

- Sports are good exercise.
- Sports keep teens busy and out of trouble.
- Sports teach teens how to work as part of a team.
- Sports are a way to make friends.
- Sports build skills and self-esteem.
- Sports teach teens how to be good winners and losers.

Girls who are in sports have better self-esteem. They get depressed less often.

Some teens get hurt doing sports. They may break bones, lose teeth, or pull muscles. Some injuries can last for a lifetime.

Some coaches and parents work teens too hard. They put too much pressure on teens to win. This can be bad for teens. Sports should be fun for teens. They should be something to look forward to.

Some teens take drugs to do better at sports. These drugs are called steroids. They make teens stronger and bigger. These drugs are bad for many reasons:

- Taking steroids is bad for the heart and liver.
- Steroids can make it so a boy can never be a father. A man who can't father a baby is called sterile.
- Steroids give girls more body hair and make their breasts smaller. These changes don't go away when the teen stops taking steroids.

Teens need some free time. Some teens do too many sports. They are too busy. They don't have time to sleep or study. They are always rushed and stressed.

What can I do?

Let your teen choose a sport. Don't push your teen to follow your dreams.

Support your teen. Go to games. Let your teen know you think sports are good. Tell your teen how proud you are.

Focus on playing fair and having fun. Don't focus on winning.

Teach your teen to be a good winner and loser. Watch how you act at your teen's games.

- Don't lose control.
- Don't use bad language.
- Don't get angry.
- Don't argue with the referee or coach.

Praise your teen after a game, even if the team lost. Don't talk about your teen's mistakes. This will make your teen feel bad. Talk about how hard everyone worked. Talk about the good plays. Your teen will learn that how a person plays the game is the most important thing.

Keep your teen safe. Make sure your teen wears the right shoes, pads, and other safety gear. Make sure the gear is in good shape.

Teach your teen to pay attention to the body's signals. Pain means something is wrong. Tell your teen to stop if something pops, hurts, or doesn't feel right.

Don't let your teen play sports when sick. A sick teen can get hurt. Teach your teen what to do for pain or a pulled muscle. Use the word RICE to remember what to do:

- **R**est the area that hurts.
- **I**ce the area for 30 minutes every 4 hours for 24 hours.
- **C**ompress or wrap the area.
- **E**levate (raise) the injured area higher than the heart.

Watch for signs that your teen is being pushed too hard. Some signs are:

- Your teen plays sports when hurt or in pain.
- Your teen is on a special diet that does not seem right to you.
- Your teen's school grades drop.
- Sports take up all your teen's time. There is little time to study or go out.
- Your teen is losing or gaining a lot of weight.

Tell your teen never to take drugs to get bigger or stronger. These drugs hurt the body for life. Watch for signs that your teen may be taking drugs to get stronger.

Teens in sports need to eat the right food. Keep lots of healthy food in the house. Help your teen pack snacks for school.

When should I get help?

- Your teen has bad pain.
- Your teen has pain or swelling that does not go away in a few days.
- Your teen is not eating right.
- Your teen is gaining or losing a lot of weight.
- Your teen is failing at school.
- Sports are the only thing your teen wants to do.

Eating Disorders

What is it?

It's an unhealthy way of eating that a teen can't stop. There are three eating problems that teens can have. They are called eating disorders.

- Eating very little food and becoming too thin. This is called **anorexia**.

- Eating large amounts of food. The teen then gets rid of the food by throwing up or taking laxatives. (These are over-the-counter medicines to help you have a BM.) This is called **bulimia**.

- Eating too much food and gaining a lot of weight. This is called **compulsive overeating**.

Did you know?

Most teens with eating problems are girls. Boys can also have eating problems. Most teens with eating problems need help from an outside expert. Without help, a teen can die.

Teens with eating problems often have few friends. They spend a lot of time alone. They worry about food and how they look.

Many teens want to look like movie stars or models. This can cause eating problems.

Teen eats too little (anorexia):

Anorexia is a very serious illness. It starts as a diet to lose a few pounds. Once the weight is lost, the teen can't stop dieting.

Anorexia often starts when a teen is young. It can go on for many years. Teens with this problem eat very little. They starve themselves to be thin. They often exercise a lot to get even thinner.

A teen with this problem looks very sick. Here are some signs:

- Teen is very thin, just skin and bones.
- Teen has dry skin and thin hair.
- Monthly period stops.
- Teen feels cold all the time.
- Fine hairs grow on the arms, back, and face.
- Teen is weak and depressed.

The teen is very thin but feels fat and is afraid of gaining weight.

A teen girl with anorexia loses her body curves. She looks like a child again. Her self-esteem is tied to how thin she is. The only thing that matters is being thin.

Teens with anorexia deny they have a problem. They are very sick. They can die without help.

Teen eats large amounts of food and throws up or takes laxatives after eating (bulimia):

Bulimia often starts in the later teen years. Teens with this problem eat a lot of food in a short time. This is called binge (binj) eating. They binge alone or with friends. Binge eating often happens when a teen feels stress. Teens also do it when they are lonely or upset.

They eat high-calorie "junk" food like ice cream and cookies. Then they feel guilty. They make themselves throw up right after eating. They do this so they won't get fat. Many teens also take laxatives to get the food out of their bodies.

It can be hard to tell that a teen has bulimia. The teen's weight often stays the same. Here are some signs to watch for:

- Trips to the bathroom right after meals
- Large amounts of food missing from the house
- Tooth decay from throwing up often
- Puffy face near the ears
- Cuts and dry skin on the hands and fingers

- Mood swings
- Muscle cramps
- Burning in the chest
- Feeling tired

Teens with bulimia know they have a problem. They try to keep it a secret. Bulimia is a serious problem. A teen can die without help.

Teen eats too much food and gets fat (compulsive overeating):

Teens with this eating problem can't limit how much food they eat. They use food to feel better. The overeating often starts as a child. Problems with weight often run in families. Heavy parents tend to have heavy children.

Sometimes teen overeating starts after something bad happens, like an accident. The teen eats too much and gets fat. The teen keeps overeating even after things are OK again.

What can I do?

Eat healthy and exercise. Teach your teen to do the same. Serve healthy foods in the right amounts.

The website www.ChooseMyPlate.gov will give you more ideas about serving healthy food. A healthy plate has the 5 food groups and how much of each group you should eat. You can use the plate to make healthy meals for you and your family.

Teens need to eat three meals and two snacks a day. They need to eat food every day from each of the five food groups.

- Grains: bread (whole grain), cereal, rice, and pasta
- Vegetables
- Fruits
- Protein: Meat, fish, poultry, beans, eggs, and nuts
- Dairy: Milk, yogurt, and cheese (low fat or nonfat)

Give your teen foods high in iron. Teens need to eat foods rich in iron, because they are growing. Girls need extra iron due to their monthly period. Some foods high in iron are:

- Meats
- Spinach
- Raisins
- Beans

- Cereals and breads with added iron

Try to eat meals together as a family. Teach your teen healthy eating habits.

Don't do these things:

- Don't make your teen eat all the food on the plate. Your teen should stop eating when full.

- Don't use food as a reward. For example, don't give extra cake for doing well on a test.

- Don't use food to make your teen feel better. When your teen is sad, talk about it. Eating doesn't help.

- Don't use food to punish your teen.

Watch for signs that your teen may have an eating disorder. Don't talk about dieting near your teen. Notice if your teen goes to the bathroom right after meals.

If you are worried, take your teen to the doctor, no matter what your teen says. Teens don't always know when they have an eating problem.

When should I get help?

- Your teen has gained or lost a lot of weight.
- Your teen refuses meals.
- Your teen is always on a diet and is afraid to gain weight.
- Your teen works out too much.
- Your teen looks sick.
- Your teen has some signs of an eating problem.
- Your teen is thin but says, "I'm fat."
- Your teen takes laxatives to go to the bathroom.

You can call the National Eating Disorder Association Helpline at 1-800-931-2237 for help.

Cutting and Self-Injury

What is it?

When strong, bad emotions cause teens to harm their own bodies.

Did you know?

Some teens hurt their own bodies. Here are some ways they do this:

- Cut their skin with scissors
- Scratch their skin deeply with fingernail
- Make burns on their body
- Hit their head against a wall
- Pick their skin with pins or other sharp things
- Pull out their hair
- Bite their arm or leg
- Break a bone

Here are some names for these acts: self-injury, self-abuse, self-harm, and self-mutilation. Teens may do this when they are stressed. They will do this as a quick way to get rid of stress.

Teens may be angry, sad, or depressed. They may worry about life and have mixed-up thoughts. Teens may think they don't look good. They may think they are not like other teens, or that they don't fit in. They may have lost a friend, a boyfriend, or a girlfriend. There may be problems in the teen's family, such as divorce, death, or trouble with family members. A teen can feel a lot of stress.

Teens have problems talking about their feelings. They don't know what to say. They have not yet learned how to handle stress. Cutting may help a teen get rid of feeling tense. Cutting becomes a habit for some teens. Every time they feel tense they go to a secret place. There, they cut themselves or do another form of self-injury.

They are usually not trying to kill themselves. These are not suicide attempts.

Self-injury will leave scars on the body for the rest of a teen's life. It will leave emotional scars you can't see. It is unhealthy. It is dangerous. There can be a loss of blood and even death.

Here are some signs that a teen is cutting:

- You see marks on the teen's body, and you wonder where they came from.

- A teen wears long sleeves and long pants even when the weather is hot.

- A teen spends a lot of time alone.

- A teen does things in secret. The teen goes alone into a bedroom, closet, or garage. At school the teen will use the restroom or some other place where no one will see the cutting.

Teens hide what they use for cutting or self-injury. They may use things like a safety pin, scissors, razor, or a sharp pen.

The Internet has helped spread cutting among teens. There are videos and blogs about cutting. There are clubs with teens who cut and do self-injury.

What can I do?

If you find out that your teen is cutting or doing self-injury, try to stay calm. Getting angry won't help. Trying to force your teen to stop will not work. Simply telling your teen to stop will not work.

Your teen needs help. Talk to your teen's doctor. Ask for a referral to someone who can help. Your teen will need to see a counselor or psychologist, social worker, or other trained person.

Here are some things you can do:

- Spend time talking to your teen. Praise your teen's looks and good actions.

- Help your teen find ways to handle stress. Try exercise, listening to music, or talking to people.

- Help your teen learn to do something else when the thought of cutting comes to mind.

- Encourage your teen to find friends who like the same fun things your teen does.

- Help your teen find a hobby, play an instrument, or enjoy the outdoors. Find things to do that will help your teen feel less tense.

When should I get help?

- Get help as soon as you know your teen is doing self-injury. Do not wait. Your teen will need professional help.

- Look for a support group in your area for teens who cut or do self-injury.

- See page 4 for a list of places you can call for help.

Anger

What is it?

Anger is a strong feeling that makes a person ready to react.

Did you know?

Anger is normal. But violence is not normal. It is not normal to be angry all the time. Many teens get angry often. Some teens have trouble controlling their anger. This can lead to harm.

Teens get angry with their parents for many reasons.

Teens learn by example. They deal with anger the way adults do. Parents need to handle their own anger. It's not easy to stay calm when a person is angry. Yelling does not help. Things said in anger can hurt a person.

Anger can cover up depression. Depressed teens may hurt themselves or others.

What can I do?

Watch for signs that your teen is angry. Talk with your teen. Talk about why your teen is angry. Help your teen find the real reason for these feelings. Your teen may feel better knowing what is wrong.

Anger

Your teen will often get angry with you. Don't give in just because your teen is angry. If you do, your teen will learn that anger gets results. It is OK to give in if you are wrong.

Teach your teen to feel the signs of getting angry. Knowing the signs can help control anger. Some things to notice are:

- Fast heartbeat and breathing
- Feeling in a bad mood
- Flushed cheeks
- A sick feeling in the stomach
- Tight muscles in the throat and chest
- Feeling the urge to hurt someone

Teach your teen good ways to deal with anger. The best way is to find the problem causing the anger and fix it. Sometimes your teen doesn't even know what the problem is. Your teen may know the problem but can't fix it.

Teach your teen by example how to handle anger and how to forgive. Here are some healthy ways to deal with anger:

- Talk about feelings with a friend or someone the teen trusts.
- Go for a walk or jog.
- Work out in a gym.
- Paint or draw.
- Write about feelings.
- Punch a bag or pillow.
- Count backwards or take deep breaths.

When should I get help?

- Your teen always seems angry.
- Your teen hits or throws things when angry.
- Your teen can't control moments of anger.
- You are afraid your teen is depressed.
- You are afraid your teen may hurt someone.
- You can't control your anger.
- You are always angry at your teen.

Violence and Bullying

What is it?

Violence is something people do to hurt themselves or someone else. It causes pain, suffering, injury, or death. Bullying is a form of violence.

Did you know?

People can do violence to people by pushing, stabbing, or holding them down. People can do violence with words, by using threats or trying to control what someone does. Violence may be sexual, where a teen is forced to do a sex act.

Teens see violence all around them. It's in movies, on TV, and in the news. Many video games are very violent. Violence may seem "normal" to your teen.

Violence of any kind is not normal or OK. There is no one act or sign to warn us that a teen may be violent. Here are some signs that your teen may be violent:

- Loses his or her temper often
- Destroys things
- Uses drugs or alcohol
- Hurts animals
- Carries knives or guns

- Gets into a lot of fights
- Has trouble with teachers or staff at school

Bullying

Bullying is when one or more teens try to make another teen feel bad. The person being bullied may feel scared, anxious, ashamed, not accepted, alone, or not safe.

Bullies pick on people to have power. Bullies may pick on a teen who gets upset easily. They may choose a teen who won't stand up to them. A bully may choose a teen who is shy, has problems at home, or is small or weak.

A bully may pick on someone who seems different:

- Wears thick glasses or odd clothes
- Is new to the school
- Is overweight
- Is disabled

Bullies may pick on someone who has a different faith. They may pick on someone because of race. They may pick on someone who is lesbian, gay, bisexual, or transgender. They may pick on someone who looks different.

Bullying does harm. The teen who is bullied suffers. Bullying will slow a teen's social and emotional growth. A teen who is bullied may not do well in school.

Violence and Bullying

Cyberbullying

Cyberbullying is when a bully uses things like these to bully:

- Cell phones
- Cell phone cameras
- Computer tablets
- Social media sites
- Chat rooms
- Text messaging
- Online game rooms

The bully posts messages, photos, or other things about a teen that hurt, insult, and are mean.

Cyberbullying can happen anytime. It's hard to get away from this kind of bully. This bully can reach a teen who is alone.

Messages from a cyberbully travel very quickly to a lot of people. You may not know who is doing it. This makes it easy for the bully to be cruel.

Deleting messages from a cyberbully is very hard to do. These messages can turn up in chat rooms, blogs, instant messages, and text messages. They may appear in emails or on sites such as YouTube and Facebook.

A teen who is cyberbullied can be angry, hurt, ashamed, and scared.

School violence

Violence in school happens as bullying, cyberbullying, arguing, fighting, gang violence, or with weapons.

Violence can happen on school property, or on the way to and from school. It can happen at school-sponsored events, or on the way to and from school-sponsored events.

Abuse

Teen abuse is violent actions by one person to gain power and control over another person.

Teen abuse happens in relationships. It can happen in families. It can happen when teens date.

Teen abuse includes name calling, hair pulling, and taking away freedom. Teen abuse can be destroying a teen's things. It can also be sex touching that the teen doesn't want.

Teens who are abused have low self-esteem. They may not do well at school. They have trouble eating, sleeping, and studying. They are angry. They are scared and feel alone. They may feel hopeless.

What can I do?

Teens need to learn how to cope with violence. Teens need help from parents, teachers, and trusted adults to do this.

Violence and Bullying

Many TV shows and video games are violent. TV shows have ads that make alcohol use seem cool. Violent sex is very common on TV.

Here are some things you can do:

- Don't let a child younger than age 10 watch violence on TV.

- Don't use your TV as a babysitter.

- Put your TV, computer, or video game box in a busy place. That way you can see how they are being used.

- Limit the amount of time your teen watches TV or plays video games to 2 hours a day.

- Don't turn on the TV before school. Turn off the TV long before bedtime.

- Teach your child to think about whether a TV program is good or bad. Is it too violent or fake?

- Find fun and smart things for your teen to do. For example, your teen can read, do hobbies, listen to music, or play sports or family board games.

Know what your teen is doing on the Internet. Here are some questions to ask and things you can do:

- What does your teen do online?

- What web sites does your teen visit?

- Try out the cell phone, tablet, or computer that your teen uses.

- Ask for your teen's passwords. Say you will use them only in an emergency.
- Tell your teen to let you know right away about being cyberbullied.

Have rules about using the Internet:

- Tell your teen not to give out personal information online.
- Keep online computer time to one hour or less.
- Tell your teen what sites are OK to visit. Bookmark these sites.
- Tell your teen to never open or send emails to a stranger.
- Tell your teen never to meet someone face-to-face after only meeting online.
- Tell your teen not to share anything that could hurt or embarrass others.
- Tell your teen to think before posting pictures. Who will see them? Tell your teen that pictures can never be removed.
- Tell your teen not to share passwords with friends.
- Tell your teen not to answer or forward cyberbullying.
- Make it clear what will happen if your teen does not follow the rules.

Know if your teen is being bullied. Here are some signs that someone is bullying your teen:

- Poor grades in school, no interest in school, or not wanting to go to school
- Change in eating habits. Your teen may come home from school hungry because of not eating lunch.
- Loss of friends. Your teen does not want to go to parties, dances, or out with other teens.
- Bruises, scratches, or injuries on the body
- Clothes may be torn
- Headaches or stomachaches, feels sick or acts sick
- Has trouble sleeping
- Loss of personal things, such as school books, jackets, shoes
- Feels bad about self
- Runs away from home. Teen may try to hurt self or talk about suicide.

Check in with your teen often. Find ways to talk to your teen. Ask about friends. Talk about school. Ask questions:

- What is lunchtime like?
- Have you ever been scared to go to school?
- What would you do if you saw a friend with a gun?

Teens need to know that being bullied is **not** their fault. Give your teen tips for dealing with bullies:

- Stay near friends who will help you.
- Move out of reach. Step out of line or change seats.
- Walk away or stay away from the bully. Don't fight back.
- Get help from a teacher, coach, or other adult.

Help your teen know what to say to the bully the next time. Practice with your teen what to say. Tell your teen to look at the bully and tell the bully to stop.

Tell your teen not to let the bully see any feelings. Tell your teen to have a buddy. Go with friends or other people to and from school, shopping, and on other trips.

Teach your teen to be calm and proud. Say:

- Walk straight, with shoulders square, chin up, and look people in the eye.
- Speak slowly and clearly.
- Keep a calm tone when you talk.

Practice a scene where a teen is bullied. Teach your teen what to say when moving away from a bully. The teen should use a normal tone of voice and say, "See you later" or "Have a nice day."

Sometimes a teen can't get away from a bully. Tell your teen, "If you can't get away, put your hands up with the palms out and say 'Stop.'"

Tell your teen to report all bullying.

Here are more things you can do if your teen is being cyberbullied:

- Tell your teen you won't take the computer away if your teen tells you about being cyberbullied.
- Write down the dates and times of the bullying. Describe it in detail.
- Save screens, emails, and text messages.
- Block the person who is cyberbullying.
- Report bullying to Internet and cell phone service centers.
- Report cyberbullying to social media sites.
- Visit social media sites to learn how to block senders and change settings. Control who can contact your teen.
- Report to police any of these things:
  - Threats
  - Sexual photos or videos (pornography)
  - Sexual messages
  - Pictures taken where you would expect privacy
  - Stalking
  - Hate crimes

Don't keep guns or weapons in your home. Lock up guns and weapons that you must keep in your home. Get help if your teen shows signs of being violent. Model how your teen should act. Teach love and caring for disabled people. Teach love and caring for people who are different.

Get to know your teen's friends. Get to know their parents. Help your teen have good friends.

If your teen is being bullied, don't wait. Get help right away. Go to school to ask for help. Find a therapist or counselor to work with your teen. Go to counseling sessions with your teen.

Here are some things to do if your teen becomes violent at home:

- Try to stay calm. Stop talking to your teen.
- Move yourself and other children away from the teen. Go to another room or leave the house.
- Call 911 if your teen is pushing, fighting, shoving, or breaking things.
- Stay in a safe area if you stay at home. Try to stay in a place where you can leave if you decide to.
- Don't talk to your teen until your teen quiets down.
- Remove any guns from your home.
- If there was no arrest you may get an At Risk Youth Petition. Your teen will have to go to counseling.

When there has been violence in your teen's school or community, talk to your teen. Be patient. Teens need to talk about their feelings. Listen to your teen. Tell your teen that these feelings are normal. Your teen may want to talk to a counselor.

Let your teen know that the area is safe. Tell your teen to report anything strange to a trusted adult. This may prevent violence.

Tell your teen that no one understands the violence that just happened. Teach your teen that violence is never the answer to any problem.

Teach your teen how to get help when there is a bully. Tell the teen to go to an adult or teacher and say, "Excuse me, I really need help." Teach your teen to touch the adult or teacher's arm when the adult or teacher does not listen. Tell your teen to keep on trying to get help.

Keep trying to help your teen. Make sure your teen knows that you care. Bullying may not stop right away. Help your teen until the bullying stops.

Don't talk to the parents of the child who is bullying. This may make things worse.

Don't try to handle teen abuse alone. Try to stay calm. Call 911 in an emergency.

Have your teen see a doctor or therapist. Look in your phone book to find help for families and victims of abuse. (See page 4 for a list of places to call.)

When should I get help?

- There have been threats of violence, sex messages or photos, stalking, or hate crimes. Call your local police.

- Your teen shows signs of being violent. Don't wait to get help. Ask your doctor to refer your teen to a therapist. These people can also help you find help: school counselors, medical and health care professionals, and people trained in counseling.

- Your teen is having trouble recovering from violence, abuse, bullying, or cyberbullying. Find professional help. Ask faith leaders, local police, school staff, or health care providers where to find help for your teen. Look for groups in your community that can help.

- If the school doesn't help with bullying or cyberbullying, talk to the school superintendent or the Department of Education.

- When you can't find out what your teen is doing on the computer or phone, get help. Find a trusted adult or family friend to help you. Find a store that fixes computers. Ask them to look at your computer for clues about what your teen is doing on the Internet.

Depression

What is it?

It is feeling sad, down, or hopeless for longer than a few hours or a day. The feeling is so strong it changes how a teen looks and acts.

Did you know?

Most teens feel sad or feel down at times. The feeling usually passes in a few hours or a day.

One in five teens is depressed. Twice as many girls as boys feel depressed at times. Girls may get depressed about their bodies and how they look. Teens may get depressed about what peers say about them on the Internet.

Teens often say, "I'm depressed" or "I'm sad." This happens for many reasons. If the mood or feeling passes in a few hours or a day, it's normal. But sometimes the sad feelings don't go away. They get deeper and go on for days and weeks. The teen may start to feel that things will never get better. This is called feeling hopeless. Teens who have real depression start to look and act differently.

Here are some signs of depression:

- Less interest in school or friends
- School grades drop

- Less interest in things teen used to like
- Is angry or mean
- Cries easily
- Eats too much or too little
- Sleeps too much or too little
- Has low energy, always tired
- Can't focus
- Does not wash or dress like before
- Spends a lot of time alone
- Complains of pains or other health problems
- May be sad after the death of a family member or friend

The death of a family member or friend is very hard for anyone. It is normal for a teen to feel sad. Teens need to know it is OK to feel sad. They need to know how to cope with grief. They need adults to help them deal with their feelings.

Teens who are depressed need outside help. Some teens need to take medicine or go to a hospital. Teens who don't get help may try to hurt themselves.

What can I do?

Talk with your teen about feelings of sadness or being upset. Talking about feelings can help your teen feel better. Sit down and talk to show you care.

Help your teen share feelings by saying things like:

- "I can see that you are hurting."
- "Tell me how you are feeling."

Show your teen that these feelings matter to you. Think back to when you were a teen and how you felt.

Teens need to know that their parents love them and want to help them. Say, "I love you" and "I'm here to help." Help your teen do everyday things. These include going to school or a movie, or meeting with friends. Help your teen eat healthy, get enough sleep, and exercise every day.

Spend time with your teen. Show that you want to understand your teen's feelings. Don't make fun of what your teen tells you. It may seem small to you, but it's a big problem to your teen. Don't get angry about what your teen says. Just listen. Control your feelings.

Tell your teen that it is OK to feel sad sometimes. These sad feelings will go away. Talk about ways your teen can feel better. Exercise can help.

Teach your teen what to do when things go wrong. Help your teen learn how to solve problems.

After the death of a family member or friend, call your local grief support group. Watch for signs that your teen is depressed (see list on pages 89–90).

When should I get help?

- Your teen is sad or depressed often.

- You are not sure if your teen's mood swings are normal.

- Your teen's appetite, sleep, or energy has changed.

- Your teen doesn't want to do anything. Your teen spends a lot of time alone, cries a lot, or is angry and mean.

- Your teen has trouble studying or is failing at school.

- Your teen is getting into trouble, using drugs or alcohol, or doing other bad things.

- You are worried about your teen.

Suicide

What is it?

Suicide is killing oneself.

Did you know?

Each year 8 out of 100 teens try to kill themselves. Suicide is the third leading cause of death among teens. Girls try suicide more often. Boys succeed in killing themselves more often. Some teens try suicide more than once.

Beware of a sudden change in a teen's mood. It could mean that the teen has decided to commit suicide. Some things can put a troubled teen at greater risk for suicide, such as:

- Divorce
- Death of a close family member or friend
- Death of a pet
- Failing at school
- Breakup with a boyfriend or girlfriend
- Using drugs or alcohol
- Getting pregnant
- Bullying
- Abuse

You can call a suicide hotline to get help right away. You can find the phone number in the phone book, or call 411.

Some teens need to be put in a hospital to stay safe.

What can I do?

Watch for signs that your teen may be at risk for suicide. Here are some signs to look for:

- Sadness that does not go away
- Anger without a clear reason
- Feels lost or alone
- Loss of interest in friends, events, and school
- Spends a lot of time alone
- Starts to give things away
- Thinks there is no way out
- Uses drugs or alcohol to feel better
- Says things like "I should kill myself," or "Nothing matters anymore"
- Listens to music about death or suicide

If your teen talks about suicide, get help right away! Believe what your teen says. Don't think that suicide can't happen in your family. Talk to your doctor about your concerns. Call the National Suicide Prevention Lifeline at 1-800-273-8255.

If you think your teen is at risk for suicide, call your doctor right away. Your teen may need medicine. Your teen may need to go to a hospital.

Tell your teen to come to you for help no matter what happened. Everyone makes mistakes. You are there to help.

When your teen comes for help, don't start yelling. Teach your teen how to fix mistakes. Don't put too much pressure on your teen. Don't make your teen feel like you can't be pleased.

Teens need to hear that they are special and they are loved. They need to hear it every day. Teach your teen that life is worth living. Help your teen:

- See the beauty in the world
- See a good future
- Find an interest
- Find ways to be happy

Spend time listening and talking with your teen. Help your teen find hope. Let your teen know there are things that can be done.

Read your teen's diary if it is left out. It may be your teen's way of asking for help. Do this only if you are worried about your teen's safety.

Spend more time with your teen. Be there when your teen comes home from school. Keep guns, kitchen knives, and all medicines (including over-the-counter medicines) in a safe place. Try to keep them in a locked cabinet or somewhere safe so teens cannot get them.

Never give up on your teen.

When should I get help?

- Your teen talks about death or suicide, or says things like "I wish I were dead."
- Your teen writes about death.
- Your teen gives things away.
- Your teen seems depressed and does not want to do anything.
- You are worried about your teen.
- You think your teen is at risk for suicide.

Teens who try to hurt themselves need help right away. Call the National Suicide Prevention Lifeline at 1-800-273-8255 or the National Hopeline Network at 1-800-442-4673. They are open 24 hours a day, 7 days a week.

Dating and Sex 4

Notes

_____

_____

_____

_____

_____

_____

_____

_____

_____

_____

_____

_____

_____

Dating

What is it?

Two teens who like each other go out and do things together.

Did you know?

Dating can mean going out with another teen to just do things together. Dating usually means two teens really like each other and have fun together. Dating may mean that a teen has promised to only do things with that teen.

Being serious about another person may not mean a promise to stay together for the future. A teen may like to have another teen to count on and do things with.

Parents should start talking to teens about dating before it starts. Teens who date begin to think about being in love at age 14 or 15.

Teens don't know how to date. They need to learn. Teens learn about dating from friends. They learn about dating on TV and the Internet. Teens need to learn about dating from their parents. It is important to talk to your teen about dating.

Teach your teen about fun and healthy dating. A teen should feel safe with another teen. Dating is a time to learn about relationships.

Abuse can happen when dating. There can be hitting, slapping, choking, name-calling, "put-downs," and unwanted sex.

Abuse is also when one teen tries to control another teen by doing any of these things:

- Never being pleased or saying nice things to the teen
- Telling the teen how to act and what to wear
- Wanting to spend all their time together
- Preventing the teen from doing things with others

Abuse is never OK.

Here are some signs that a teen may be in an abusive relationship:

- Teen is afraid to break up.
- There are many phone calls or texts every day from the person teen is dating.
- There are marks on the teen's body for no known reason.

Serious dating or doing a lot of dating can be a problem. A teen may have poor grades in school, use drugs, and have sex. This may mean a teen has fewer friends.

Parents should have rules for dating. Here are some rules you might have:

- A date should be no more than 1 year older or 1 year younger than your teen.

- No alcohol or drugs on a date.

- Set a time to be home after a date.

- Decide where a teen can go on a date.

Rules help teens say "no" to a date for something they do not want to do.

Sexting is sending naked and sex photos or sex text messages. This is done with a cell phone, computer, tablet, or other device. Videos also may be used in sexting. Tell your teen sexting is never OK.

Make sure your teen is mature enough to have a cell phone, computer, or other device. Tell your teen that once photos and messages are sent on the Internet they are there for all the world to see forever.

Tell your teen not to forward sexts to someone else. Teens should talk to a parent, trusted adult, school teacher, or staff about any sexts they get.

Sexting is dangerous. It can lead to cyberbullying. Your teen may become involved in child pornography. In some places sexting is illegal.

What can I do?

Read these chapters in this book to help you talk to your teen about dating:

- Rape and Date Rape, pages 105–106
- Not Having Sex (Abstinence), pages 107–109
- Sex, pages 110–113

- Safer Sex, pages 114–118
- Sexually Transmitted Diseases (STDs), pages 119–122
- Birth Control, pages 127–134

Parenting classes or programs are held by most schools or in your community.

Be warm and caring when you talk to your teen about dating. Talk openly with your teen about dating, love, and sex. Let your teen know what you think about dating.

Try to get your teen to do the right things when dating. Try to talk quietly. Don't come on too strong. You don't want your teen to take a stand against what you think.

Talk about:
- Sex
- The good and bad about dating
- Your dating rules
- That "no" means **no**
- No drugs or alcohol on a date
- What to do if your teen is on a date and wants to come home
- What to do if a date doesn't take "no" for an answer

Get to know your teen's girlfriends and boyfriends. Help your teen think of fun things to do on a date. Talk with your teen about who will pay for the date. It may be a good idea to have both teens share the cost. Offer to be the driver if your teen doesn't drive yet.

Here are other things to do before your teen goes on a date:

- Get the phone number of the other teen's parents.
- Get the address of where the date will be.
- If possible, give your teen a cell phone.
- Have a code question or word that your teen can use to get your help.

Make sure your teen has money to call you or to take a bus or taxi home. Tell your teen what time to be home. Make it early at first. You can change the time as your teen gets older, or for special dates like a school dance. Tell your teen to call you if the date will end later than planned.

Try to be there when your teen comes home from a date. Talk with your teen about how things went. Don't be too pushy.

Give your teen rules to follow with online (Internet) strangers and "friends":

- Don't send pictures.
- Don't describe who you are, where you live, or where you go to school.
- Don't meet someone in person that you have only met online. If you want to meet the person, make sure a parent is with you. Meet in a public place, like a coffee house.
- Teens should always tell an adult if someone online wants to meet in person.

If your teen is dating someone you don't like, talk with your teen about it. Tell your teen why you don't like this person.

Older teens may not want to talk with you about their dates. This is part of becoming an adult.

When should I get help?

- You are not ready to talk to your teen about dating.

- Your teen is dating a person you think will get your teen into trouble. You tried talking with your teen, but the dating still goes on.

- Your teen is younger than 15 years old and talks of love and marriage.

- Your teen is sad (depressed) all the time, after breaking up with another teen.

- You see signs of violent or controlling behavior in your teen or in your teen's relationship.

You can call the National Teen Dating Abuse Helpline (Love is Respect) at 1-866-331-9474.

Rape and Date Rape

What is it?

Rape is when one person forces another person to have sex. Date rape is when you are forced to have sex by someone you know. It can happen on a date or at a party. It's also rape if a person has sex with someone who is too drunk or high on drugs to know what is happening.

Did you know?

Rape is a crime. A person who rapes someone can go to jail. It is never OK to rape someone. People don't "ask" to be raped by the clothes they wear or the way they act.

If a person says "no" to sex, the other person should stop. Teens need to be taught that "no" means no. A person can say "no" at any time. Heavy kissing and touching doesn't mean a teen wants to have sex.

Some teens may think they should get sex in return for paying for a date. This is not true. Teens should talk before a date about who will pay. Sex is not a way to pay someone back.

There are drugs that can be put in a person's drink. A person who takes the drug can be raped without knowing it. These drugs are called date rape drugs. They also may be called "roofies."

A person who is raped needs help from a doctor, nurse, or social worker. The person must not shower, wash, or change clothes before seeing a doctor. Rape crisis centers help people who have been raped. You can find the phone number in the phone book or call 411.

What can I do?

Talk with your teen about rape and date rape.

To avoid rape, teach your teen these things:
- Have first dates in a group or in a public place.
- Make sure no one puts anything in your drink.
- Don't drink alcohol or take drugs.
- Don't let your date get drunk or take drugs.
- Stay with other people at parties. Don't go off alone with your date.
- Bring money so you can call home or take a bus or taxi.
- Talk to your date about sex. Agree that if one person says "no," it means **no**.

Boys and girls can be charged with statutory rape and go to jail if they have sex with someone under the legal age (16 or 18 depending on the state). This can happen even if the person under age agrees to have sex.

When should I get help?

If a teen is raped, take the teen to a hospital right away. Tell the teen, "This is not your fault." Make sure the teen does not shower, wash, or change clothes before going to the hospital. Call the National Sexual Assault Hotline (RAINN) at 1-800-656-4673 for help. They are open 24 hours a day, 7 days a week.

Not Having Sex (Abstinence)

What is it?

Abstinence means not having sex.

Did you know?

Not having sex is 100% safe in preventing pregnancy. It is almost 100% safe in preventing sexually transmitted diseases (STDs).

It may be hard for a teen not to have sex. Friends may say they are having sex. But this may not be true. Teens may feel they are in love. They may want to have sex because of these feelings.

Teens see sex on TV and in the movies. Teens need a lot of support not to have sex. They need people to say it's OK not to have sex.

Not having sex keeps a teen:
- Free from worry about getting pregnant
- Free from sexually transmitted diseases (STDs)
- Free from loss of self-respect
- Free to have lots of friends of both sexes
- Able to focus on sports, work, and school

Not Having Sex (Abstinence)

Teens who had sex can decide not to have sex again. Many churches, temples, and other places of worship have support groups for teens who don't want to have sex.

Sex does not make a teen part of an "in" group. It does not help a teen keep friends or stop feeling lonely.

There are many ways teens can show they care, like:

- Hugs and kisses
- Holding hands
- Talking about feelings
- Writing love poems or letters
- Buying each other gifts
- Talking on the phone
- Doing things together, like working out

What can I do?

Talk with your teen about not having sex. Tell your teen that not having sex is OK. Teach your teen about condoms and birth control. Teens who don't plan to have sex still need to know about these things.

Talk with your teen about sex. Ask how your teen feels about it. Plan what you will say if your teen asks you what you did as a teen. Share what you learned from your actions. Talk about other ways that teens can show they care.

Help your teen find a support group. Talk with your teen about how to say "no" to sex. Here are some things your teen can say:

- "I'm not ready to have sex."
- "Please respect my choice not to have sex."
- "If you are only going out with me to have sex, let's stop seeing each other now."
- "If you love me, you wouldn't want me to do something I'm not ready for."
- "I don't care if everybody is doing it. I'm not ready."
- "Even though I had sex with you before, I made a mistake. I don't want to have sex again."

Spend time with your teen. Do things together. Show your teen that there are lots of fun things to do.

Don't accuse your teen of having sex because of something you heard.

When should I get help?

Call your local church, place of worship, or community groups. Ask about groups and events that support teens who do not want to have sex.

You can call the Abstinence Clearinghouse at 1-888-577-2966 for help.

Sex

What is it?

Sex is the act of putting the penis into the vagina. This is also called intercourse. Oral sex is when the penis is put into the mouth or the mouth is put over a girl's genitals. If the penis is put in the anus, it is called anal sex. Here are other words for sex:

- Getting laid
- Going all the way
- Doing it
- Going to bed
- Making love
- Hooking up
- Sleeping with someone

Coitus and copulation also mean sex.

Did you know?

Teens see sex on TV and in the movies. It's in music, books, and other places. Teens need to learn the facts about sex. It's good to begin talking to children about sex at the age of 8 or 9, before their bodies start to change.

Teens need to know about sex, birth control, and sexually transmitted diseases (STDs) before they start to date or have sex. Talking about sex does not make teens want to have sex.

Most schools have sex education classes that teach the facts about sex. Parents need to talk with teens about when it is right and wrong to have sex, and about saying no to sex.

Teens often learn about sex from their friends. What they learn may not be right.

Many teens have sex before they are ready. Here are some reasons this happens:

- They don't know how to say no to sex.
- They are afraid of being different.
- Their friends talk them into having sex. This is called peer pressure.
- They want to please their date or prove their love.

Many teens who had sex wish they had not.

Here are some questions for teens who are thinking about having sex:

- Do you feel different because you never had sex?
- Do you know how to protect yourself from pregnancy and STDs?
- Are you being pressured into having sex?
- Will having sex change how you feel about yourself?

What can I do?

Read this book to learn what to say to your teen about sex. Be open and honest with your child about sex from a young age. Always answer your teen's questions. Make it

OK to ask questions. Make it OK to talk about sex. Don't lecture about sex. Use the right words for body parts.

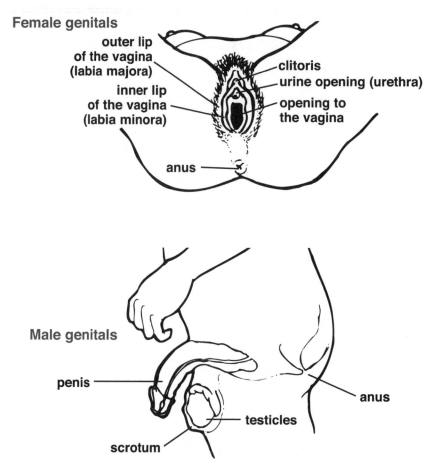

Female genitals

outer lip
of the vagina
(labia majora)

inner lip
of the vagina
(labia minora)

clitoris

urine opening (urethra)

opening to
the vagina

anus

Male genitals

penis

anus

testicles

scrotum

Start talking with your teen about sex. Ask questions like:

- What are you learning in school about sex?
- What are your friends saying about sex?
- What do you know about STDs?
- Is anyone making you have sex?

There are many groups that teach about sex. You and your teen can join one together. Your church or place of worship may have a teen and parent group. The YMCA or the local Boys and Girls Club may have groups.

Help your teen plan what to say when being pushed into having sex:

* "Stop! I want to go home now!"
* "I'm not ready to have sex."
* "Don't push me to have sex with you. I don't want to."
* "I don't need to prove my love by having sex."
* "If you love me, you will wait."

Tell your teen that it's normal to dream about sex. It's OK to talk about sex. Explain that sex does not help anyone fit in or be cool.

When should I get help?

* You don't understand some things about sex.
* You don't feel that you can talk with your teen about sex.
* Your teen is having sex. You want birth control for your teen.
* You want your teen checked for STDs or pregnancy. The visit is private between the doctor and your teen. The doctor can't talk to you about the visit unless your teen says it's OK.

Safer Sex

What is it?

Safer sex means using a
condom during vaginal,
anal, and oral sex. This
keeps the man's sperm from
going inside the partner. It
also keeps body fluids away
from each other.

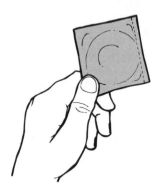

Did you know?

Here are some other names people use for condoms:

- Rubber
- Love glove
- Safe
- Sheath
- Trojan
- Balloon

A condom should be put on as soon as the penis is hard.
Condoms help stop the spread of most STDs (sexually
transmitted diseases). Condoms work only when used the
right way. Using a condom every time is each person's
duty.

Many people who have an STD don't know it. They don't have any signs. They look and feel well.

Condoms are not good forever. There is a date on the outside wrapper. Check the date before using the condom. If the date has passed, the condom won't work. You should throw it away.

Here's how to put on a condom:

Step 1 Squeeze the center of the condom package to get the air out. If there is no air, the condom is no good. Throw it away.

Step 2 Open the package with care. Be sure not to tear the condom with your nails or teeth.

Step 3 Men with a foreskin should pull back the foreskin first.

Step 4 Put the condom over the tip of the penis. Make sure the ring of the condom is on the outside.

Step 5 Squeeze the air out of the tip of the condom. Hold the tip of the condom with one hand. Unroll the condom to the base of the penis with the other hand.

If the condom does not unroll, it's on wrong. Throw it away. Start over with a new condom.

After sex, hold the condom and pull the penis out slowly. Slide the condom off. Throw away the condom. Never use the same condom more than one time. Don't use two condoms at the same time. It is not as safe as one condom.

Latex condoms are best. Don't use lambskin condoms. They don't protect against STDs. Some people are allergic to latex. Signs of allergy are redness, itching, and burning. People who are allergic to latex can use plastic condoms.

Some condoms have a gel in them that kills sperm. It is called a spermicide. There are creams to put in the vagina that also have spermicide. They are good to use with a condom.

Some people are allergic to spermicides. Put a little bit on the inside of your wrist to test it. Redness or itching after a few hours is a sign of allergy. If you are allergic to spermicide, don't use it.

You can use a water-based lubricant like K-Y jelly with a condom. Don't use anything oily or greasy. Don't use Vaseline, baby oil, or hand lotion with condoms. They can make condoms break.

You can buy condoms at drugstores, grocery stores, and other places. Condoms cost between $.20 and $2.50 each. Some public health clinics give away free condoms.

Keep condoms in a cool, dry place like a purse or shirt pocket. Don't keep condoms in a car or in a wallet.

Condoms don't stop all diseases. A person can still get lice, scabies, genital warts, or herpes while using a condom.

A dental dam should be used for oral sex (mouth-to-vagina or mouth-to-anus sex). A dental dam is a thin piece of latex you put over the vagina or anus. Condoms should be used for mouth-to-penis sex.

What can I do?

Learn as much as you can about safer sex. Teach your teen the right way to use a condom. Have your teen practice putting a condom on a banana.

Teach your teen that using a condom is each person's duty. Girls can buy condoms as well as boys. Go with your teen to buy the first condom. Make sure the condoms are latex and are low cost or free from a clinic.

There are many types of condoms. Tell your teen to try several types. Your teen will find the one that works best.

Talk with your teen about safe things to do:
- Kissing with closed lips
- Hugging
- Rubbing against each other with clothes on
- Masturbating alone

Teach your teen what to say and do if a partner does not want to use a condom. Teach your teen to always use a condom. Sex without a condom is a big mistake!

Teach your teen these things about condoms:

- Condoms protect against pregnancy and most STDs.
- Use a condom each time you have sex.
- A condom may break.
- Use a new condom each time.
- Carry a condom with you.
- Check the date on the outside wrapper. Don't use condoms after the date on the wrapper.
- Condoms that are good have air inside the package. Throw away the condom if there is no air.
- Know how to put a condom on the right way.
- Put a condom on as soon as the penis is hard.

Tell your teen what to do if a condom breaks:

- Stop having sex right away.
- Take the penis out.
- Take the morning-after pill within 3 days. (Read about emergency birth control on pages 132–133.)

When should I get help?

- Your teen may have an STD.
- You don't feel right talking with your teen about safer sex.
- You can't answer some of your teen's questions.
- You are worried about what your teen is doing.
- Your teen had sex, and the condom broke or came off.
- You think your teen may be pregnant.

Sexually Transmitted Diseases (STDs)

What is it?

STDs are diseases or infections. They spread from one person to another during sexual contact. Sexual contact means vaginal, oral, or anal sex. It also is skin-to-skin contact of the sex parts. Another term for STD is STI (sexually transmitted infection).

Did you know?

There are about 25 different STDs. About 3 million teens get an STD each year.

People with STDs often look fine. They may not know they have an STD. They can give the STD to a person during sex. You can get an STD during vaginal, anal, or oral sex. You can also get some STDs, like genital warts, from skin-to-skin contact.

STDs are spread by body fluids such as blood, vaginal fluids, and semen. You can get an STD the first time you have sex with someone who has it, even if that person doesn't come. You can get the same STD many times. Some STDs like chlamydia, gonorrhea, and syphilis can be cured.

Sexually Transmitted Diseases (STDs)

There is no cure for these STDs:

- HIV/AIDS
- Genital herpes
- HPV/Genital warts
- Hepatitis B

Here is a list of common STDs:

- Chlamydia
- Genital herpes
- HPV/Genital warts
- Gonorrhea
- Hepatitis B
- HIV/AIDS
- Trichomoniasis
- Crabs
- Syphilis

Here are some signs of STDs:

- Pain or itching in the genitals or sex parts
- Fluid (drip or discharge) coming out of the vagina or penis
- Burning or itching when peeing
- Sores, blisters, bumps, or rashes on the sex parts
- Fever, body aches, lower stomach pain
- Bad smell from the sex parts

People must go to the doctor right away if they think they have an STD. Here is what can happen if a person doesn't get medicine for an STD:

- Boys and girls can get sterile. This means they can never make babies or have babies.
- HPV/Genital warts can cause cancer in women.
- STDs can cause problems when a woman is pregnant.
- STDs can be passed to newborn babies.
- People can die from some STDs.

Teens who have sex must always use a condom. They also need to get tested for STDs every 6 months. Most clinics will test teens for STDs without a parent's consent.

There is a shot for hepatitis B. All teens need to get this shot. There is a shot for HPV. It protects against some types of HPV. Teens need to get the shot before they start having sex. The HPV shot can prevent cervical cancer.

What can I do?

Learn as much as you can about STDs. Talk with your teen about sex and STDs. Experts say to start when your child is 8 or 9 years old.

Answer your teen's questions honestly. Have your teen read about STDs. Talk with your teen about STDs. Show your teen pictures of some STDs. This will help your teen know why using a condom is so important.

Support your teen not to have sex. Teach your teen how to have safer sex. Here are some ways to have safer sex:

- Hug and touch each other with clothes on
- Use a condom and cream with spermicide
- Use a condom or a dental dam

Tell your teen never to do these things:

- Sex without a condom

- Oral sex without a condom or dental dam
- Share sex toys like vibrators

Some health clinics give away free condoms. Visit one near you to find out about their services.

Spend time with your teen so you can talk together. Get your teen interested in sports and other things. Never tease your teen about sex or STDs. Keep secrets that your teen tells you.

If your teen is having sex, tell your teen to get tested for STDs every 6 months. If you think your teen has an STD, take your teen to the doctor right away. Make sure your teen tells sex partners about the STD. Your teen must not have sex until the STD is treated.

Make sure your teen gets a shot for hepatitis B. Talk to your doctor about the HPV shot. Your teen needs to get the shot before starting to have sex.

When should I get help?

- Your teen is having sex and has signs of an STD (see list on page 120).
- You don't understand STDs. You want someone to talk with your teen.
- Your teen has an STD. You are worried about your teen.
- You don't feel right talking with your teen about condoms and STDs.
- Your teen needs to get a shot for HPV and hepatitis B.

HIV/AIDS

What is it?

HIV is a virus that causes AIDS. HIV and AIDS make the body weak, so it can't fight disease. People with HIV or AIDS can get sick very easily. First a person gets HIV. Months or years later, HIV causes the disease called AIDS. There is no cure for HIV or AIDS.

Did you know?

AIDS is a bad disease. People can protect themselves from getting it. People get HIV when body fluid with HIV enters the body. This fluid can be blood, semen (the liquid that sperm is in), vaginal fluid, or breast milk.

HIV is passed from person to person in these ways:

- Having oral, anal, or vaginal sex without a condom with a person who has HIV, even if you don't come.
- Using the same needle or syringe as a person with HIV.
- An infected mother can pass HIV to her unborn baby.
- A mother with HIV can pass the virus to her baby by breast-feeding.
- Body piercing and tattooing using tools with the HIV virus on them.

People with HIV can look healthy for a long time. You can't tell if people have HIV just by looking at them.

Even a person with no signs of HIV can pass along the disease. You can't get HIV by shaking hands, working, playing, or living together. You can't get HIV from food, water, bugs, or toilet seats.

Anyone can get HIV and AIDS. Movie stars, doctors, teachers, children, and teens get HIV and AIDS.

Early signs of HIV can be:

- Fever
- Feeling sick
- Swollen glands
- Sore throat
- Loose, watery BMs (diarrhea)
- Rash
- Feeling tired
- Joint and muscle pains

Other diseases can also cause these signs. The only way to be sure is to get tested for HIV.

A person with HIV can get AIDS in a few months. But some people live with HIV for 10 to 15 years before getting AIDS.

AIDS causes problems like weight loss, diarrhea, and fever. People with AIDS often get bad diseases like TB (tuberculosis), pneumonia, or cancer.

As soon as someone gets HIV, that person can pass it to others. There are tests that check for HIV and AIDS. A person can get a test at a doctor's office or a health clinic. Some tests take 15 minutes to get results. Some tests take up to 2 weeks to get the results. A person can be tested without anyone knowing. Some clinics don't ask for your name.

There is no cure for HIV and AIDS. There is medicine to slow down the disease. These medicines cost a lot of money. Public health clinics or AIDS groups can help with the cost. It is important to find out early if a person has HIV. That person needs to take medicine right away. The medicine can keep a person healthy for a longer time.

Having an STD makes it easier to get HIV. People who are having sex should get tested for STDs every 6 months.

What can I do?

Teach your teen about HIV and AIDS. Explain why using a condom is so important. Encourage your teen to be 100% safe by doing these things:

- Not having sex (see pages 107–109)
- Closed-mouth kissing
- Hugging and rubbing against each other with clothes on
- Masturbating alone

Teach your teen about safer sex (see pages 114–118).

Teach your teen to be kind to people who have HIV or AIDS. Tell your teen that you can't get AIDS by just being with a person who has AIDS.

If your teen is having sex, make sure your teen is tested for STDs every 6 months. Get help right away if your teen uses IV drugs. These are drugs that users put into the body with a needle.

When should I get help?

- Your teen has signs of HIV or AIDS (see list on page 124).

- Your teen needs to be tested for HIV or AIDS.

- You are having trouble talking with your teen about HIV. You want someone to talk with your teen.

- Your teen uses or shares needles to take drugs.

If you have questions about HIV or AIDS, call AIDS Info at 1-800-448-0440 or CDC AIDS and STD Info Hotline at 1-800-232-4636.

Birth Control

What is it?

Birth control is things people do to keep from getting pregnant. Birth control is also called contraception.

Did you know?

Not having sex is called abstinence. Not having sex is 100% safe against getting pregnant. There are a lot of birth control methods that teens can use. Teens who use birth control can still get pregnant. There is still a small chance of getting pregnant with any birth control. Without birth control, a girl can get pregnant the first time she has sex. She can get pregnant any time of the month, even during her period.

Here are things some people think will keep them from getting pregnant. **These things <u>don't</u> work. A teen can still get pregnant:**

- Standing up after sex
- Having sex on days when a woman is less likely to get pregnant. This is called the rhythm method. This is not safe.
- Pulling out of the vagina before the man's semen comes out. Many teens do this. It is not safe. This doesn't work, because a boy will leak sperm before he comes (ejaculates).

Birth Control

Here are some things that are true about birth control:

- Family planning clinics will give birth control to teens.
- Birth control is the duty of both the girl and the boy. They should talk about it before having sex.

Think about these things when choosing a form of birth control:

- How easy is it to use?
- How much does it cost?
- Is the teen taking medicine that will keep some types of birth control from working?

Teens must **always use a condom** along with another form of birth control. Here is a list of birth control methods used by many teens:

Condom or rubber

Always use a condom even when using other forms of birth control. The condom helps prevent STDs. (See pages 114–118 for how to use a condom.)

Birth control pill

It is also called the Pill. It's a very good way to keep from getting pregnant. A girl must use some other birth control the first month she starts the Pill. A doctor must write an order for birth control pills. A girl must not take someone else's pills. She must take the Pill at the same time every day, or as told by the doctor.

If a girl misses taking a pill, she needs to:

- Take it as soon as she remembers. She can take two pills on the same day.

- Use another form of birth control until she has her period. She can use spermicides with a condom.

Your teen may have side effects with the Pill. Some side effects are feeling like throwing up, sore breasts, gaining weight, headaches, swelling, and light bleeding. These often go away in a few months. There are many types of birth control pills. Each has different side effects. The doctor will find the best one for each teen.

Some teens take the Pill to make their period happen at the same time each month or for other health reasons. Birth control pills don't protect against STDs (sexually transmitted diseases). You still need to use a condom.

Depo-Provera

It's a shot that prevents pregnancy for about 12 weeks. Side effects are changes in a girl's period, gaining weight, and headaches. These often go away in a few months. A teen can get the shot at a doctor's office or family planning clinic. Depo-Provera does not protect against STDs. You still need to use a condom.

Diaphragm

It's a small cup made of soft rubber. A girl puts it in her vagina before sex. It stops sperm from going into the womb (uterus).

You need to use spermicide with a diaphragm. Spermicides kill sperm and prevent pregnancy.

Here's how to use a diaphragm:

> **Step 1** Put spermicide cream or jelly around the rim and on both sides of the diaphragm.
>
> **Step 2** Squeeze the rim of the diaphragm together.
>
> **Step 3** Push the diaphragm high up the vagina until it covers the cervix. The cervix feels like a bump under the middle of the diaphragm.

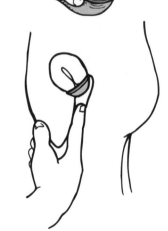

You must leave the diaphragm in the vagina for 8 hours after sex. If a girl has sex again during this time she must put more spermicide into the vagina. Don't take out the diaphragm!

A girl needs to be fitted for a diaphragm at a doctor's office or health clinic. A girl can't use another girl's diaphragm.

A girl needs to get a new diaphragm every year. She also needs a new one if she gains or loses more than 10 pounds. A diaphragm does not protect against STDs. You still need to use a condom.

Spermicides

Spermicides are medicines you put into the vagina to kill sperm. They come in many forms, like foams, jellies, creams, tablets, and suppositories. It must be put into the vagina 15 to 20 minutes before sex. Spermicides don't prevent pregnancy by themselves. They work best with another form of birth control like the diaphragm.

Read all instructions that come with spermicides before using. Don't wash spermicides out of the vagina after sex. They kill sperm for many hours.

Spermicides are sold in drugstores. Some health clinics give them away for free. Some people are allergic to spermicides. They get burning in the vagina or penis. If you are allergic, use condoms and lubricants without spermicides.

Spermicides don't protect against STDs. You still need to use a condom.

Hormonal Implant

If your teen can't remember to take the Pill, she might try a hormonal implant. The implant is a small plastic tube about the size of a matchstick. A doctor places it under the skin of the upper arm. It works for 3 years.

A teen must not smoke when using a hormonal implant. Some medicines and herbal supplements can't be taken, either. Ask your doctor which ones. A doctor can remove the implant at any time.

Hormonal implants don't protect against STDs. You still need to use a condom.

IUD (intrauterine device)

A doctor puts the IUD in place. It is a T-shaped piece of plastic placed inside the uterus. It does not let the sperm reach the egg.

The doctor or nurse will teach the teen how to check to make sure the IUD is in place. IUDs usually stay in place for 10 years. A doctor can remove the IUD at any time.

IUDs don't protect against STDs. You still need to use a condom.

Emergency Birth Control

If a girl has sex without birth control, there is still something she can do. But she must act fast. There is a pill she can take not to get pregnant after having sex. It is called the morning-after pill.

Use the morning-after pill:

- After sex without birth control
- After rape
- If a condom breaks

The girl must take it within 72 hours after sex.

You can get the morning-after pill from a drugstore without a doctor's order. The morning-after pill does not protect against STDs.

What can I do?

Learn about different forms of birth control so you can answer your teen's questions. Teach your teen about birth control. Your teen needs to know about birth control even if your teen doesn't plan to have sex.

Learning about birth control won't make your teen want to have sex. It helps your teen make good choices.

Talk about STDs along with birth control. (See pages 119–122.) Be open and honest with your teen. Start talking with your teen at a young age.

Go with your teen to get birth control if your teen asks you to. Help your teen choose the best birth control. Help pay for it, if needed. Take your teen to a free clinic for birth control if you can't pay for it. Help your teen pick another kind of birth control if one kind isn't working out.

What if your teen's partner doesn't want to use birth control? Help your teen plan what to say if the partner doesn't want to use a condom.

Never tease your teen about birth control. If your teen talks to you about birth control, don't tell anyone. It is private between you and your teen.

Your teen may get birth control without telling you. If you find out:

- Stay calm. Don't get angry.
- Don't tell your teen not to use birth control. Your teen may be having sex or thinking about it.
- Make sure your teen is using birth control the right way.
- Talk about why it is important to always use condoms.

When should I get help?

- You think your teen is pregnant.
- You can't talk with your teen about birth control. You want someone to explain it to your teen.
- Your teen won't listen to you.
- Your teen is having sex with many people.
- Your teen uses only the morning-after pill for birth control.
- Your teen has sex without a condom.
- You can't afford to pay for birth control.

Teen Pregnancy

What is it?

Pregnancy happens when a boy's sperm meets a girl's egg after sex. The sperm fertilizes the egg. The fertilized egg attaches to the uterus and grows into a baby.

Did you know?

The U.S. has nearly the highest teen pregnancy rate in the world. Two of every three teen mothers are not married.

Most teen pregnancies are not planned.

A girl can get pregnant the first time she has sex if she does not use birth control. Many teens think this can't happen to them. Only 1 in 7 teens gets birth control before starting to have sex. Here are some reasons:

- Teens don't want people to know they are having sex.
- Teens don't know where to get birth control.
- Teens don't have money to pay for it.
- Teens don't have a way to get to the doctor, clinic, or store.

Some boys feel birth control is the girl's duty. This is not true. It is the duty of both.

Some teens know about birth control but still get pregnant. Here are some reasons:

- They think they won't get pregnant.
- They didn't plan to have sex.
- They didn't have birth control with them.
- One partner does not want to use birth control.

A missed period is often the first sign of pregnancy. A teen needs to have a pregnancy test if she had sex and misses a period. She can get tested at a doctor's office or family planning clinic. The test at the clinic may be free.

Here are some other signs of pregnancy:

- Feeling sick to the stomach (nausea)
- Throwing up. This is called morning sickness.
- Sore breasts
- Feeling tired
- Gaining weight

Prenatal care is the health care a girl needs to have a healthy baby. It is very important to start prenatal care during the first month of pregnancy. There are many places to get prenatal care. A teen can go to a doctor's office or a public health clinic.

Getting pregnant affects a teen's life forever. Here are some things that can happen:

- Teen drops out of school.
- She can't get a good job.
- She makes very little money.

Teen fathers also have problems. They often drop out of school. Some teens marry because the girl got pregnant. They have a high breakup rate. There are schools and programs to help teens who are pregnant.

What can I do?

Talk with your child at an early age about sex. Talk about why it is important to protect against pregnancy and STDs (sexually transmitted diseases).

Talk with your teen about not having sex. (See pages 107–109.) Tell your teen that no one needs to have sex to fit in or be cool. If your teen girl is having sex, take her to a doctor or clinic for birth control. Teach your teen to use birth control every time she has sex.

Talk with your teen girl about what would happen if she got pregnant. Talk with your teen boy about what would happen if he got a girl pregnant. What good things in life would change? What would the future look like?

Know the signs that your teen may be pregnant. Take your teen to the doctor if you think she may be pregnant. Teach your teen that taking drugs, drinking, or smoking will hurt the baby inside her.

A pregnant teen has choices to make. Help your teen to make the right choice. These choices change a teen's life forever. Speak with the father about his wishes, too. Before she decides, a teen girl needs to know all her choices:

Stay pregnant and keep the baby.

The teen needs to know what being a parent means. It is forever. She needs to know how much it costs to raise a child. She needs to know how her life will change.

End the pregnancy. This is called abortion.

Abortion is an operation a doctor does at a clinic or office. Having an abortion can affect a teen's feelings for her whole life. Never talk a teen into or out of having an abortion. If your teen is thinking about abortion, help her find a family planning clinic or other local agency.

Abortion laws vary by state. Most states let teens have an abortion without asking a parent. Public health or family planning clinics can tell you where to get an abortion.

Have the baby, and give the baby up for adoption.

A nurse, doctor, or health clinic can tell you about adoption and how to do it. Many churches, other places of worship, and local agencies can help with adoption. The hospital can also help if a teen wants to put her baby up for adoption.

If your teen is pregnant, help her have a healthy baby by doing these things:

- See a doctor during the first month of pregnancy.
- Take a vitamin each day ordered by the doctor.
- Do not smoke, drink alcohol, or use drugs.
- Eat healthy foods.

- Stay active.
- Get lots of rest.

A teen may have to stop going to school or work when her due date gets close. Help your teen do the right things so she has a healthy baby.

When should I get help?

- Your teen started having sex.
- Your teen needs to get birth control.
- You think your teen is pregnant.

If your pregnant teen uses drugs, alcohol, or smokes, tell the doctor. These things will hurt the baby.

Get help if your teen is pregnant and has these signs:
- Bleeding
- Swelling of the face or legs
- Fast weight gain
- Bad headaches
- Trouble peeing

A new baby needs to go to the doctor for shots and checkups. It is very important to keep all doctor visits.

To get help with teen pregnancy, you can call these places:
- Planned Parenthood   1-800-230-7526
- America's Pregnancy Helpline   1-800-672-2296
- Birthright Pregnancy Helpline 1-800-550-4900

Masturbation

What is it?

Masturbation is touching your own sex parts (genitals) for sexual pleasure.

Did you know?

A lot of people masturbate, even married people. There is nothing wrong with masturbating. It does not do bad things to a person. It is a safe form of sex. A person can't get pregnant or an STD from masturbating. It lets a teen release sexual tension without having sex.

Two people can touch each other's sex parts. This is called mutual masturbation.

What can I do?

Tell your teen that masturbation is normal. Don't make your teen feel guilty about it. Tell your teen that it is private. Your teen should not do it in public.

When should I get help?

- Your teen is masturbating in public.
- Your teen feels guilty about masturbating or is depressed about it.

Sexual Abuse and Incest

What is it?

Sexual abuse is when one person forces another person to do a sex act. There are many kinds of sexual abuse. It includes when someone makes another person touch them or talk to them in a sexual way. It can happen when one person forces another person to have sex. (You can read about rape and date rape on pages 105–106.)

Incest is when a family member has sex with or touches another family member in a sexual way. Family members can be parents, stepparents, grandparents, uncles, aunts, cousins, brothers, and sisters.

Did you know?

Sexual abuse and incest are against the law. They are **never OK**. You must report them to the police. Some things put a family at higher risk for sexual abuse and incest:

- Alcohol or drug abuse in adults
- Many people living together in a small place
- A lot of stress in the family
- History of abuse or incest in the family

Sexual Abuse and Incest

People need outside help to deal with sexual abuse or incest. Sexual abuse or incest can hurt a teen for life. The teen needs help. The teen needs to talk about what happened with a social worker, therapist, or someone the teen trusts.

Sexual abuse or incest can happen to boys and girls at any age. It is never the teen's fault. Many children are afraid to tell anyone what happened because:

- They think they did something wrong.
- They think no one will believe them.
- They were told something bad will happen if they tell anyone.

Here are some signs to look out for:

- Child knows too much about sex for a child at that age.
- Child always touches his or her own sex parts.
- Child acts in a way that's not normal for a child at that age.
- Child acts out or is very angry.
- Child has bad dreams.
- Child touches other children in a sexual way.
- Child has an STD (sexually transmitted disease).
- Child tries to stay away from a certain family member.
- Child runs away from home.
- Child has headaches or other problems.
- Child cries a lot.

What can I do?

Know the signs of sexual abuse and incest. Talk to your teen about everything. Listen to what your teen says. If your teen tells you something is happening, believe it. Get help right away if you think your child was abused. Your child comes first.

When should I get help?

Get help if you think sexual abuse or incest is happening. The entire family may need help. There are many community groups that can help you.

Call the National Sexual Assault Hotline (RAINN) at 1-800-656-4673 or the Childhelp National Child Abuse Hotline at 1-800-422-4453 for help.

Homosexuality (Gay)

What is it?

Homosexuality is a strong attraction to people of the same sex. Other words for homosexual are gay and lesbian.

Did you know?

We don't know why some people are gay and others are not. It is not a disease or mental illness. Gay people lead normal lives.

It is normal for teens to be attracted to teens of the same sex. This can happen during the early teen years. This does not mean the teen is gay.

Teens like to try new things. Some teens have sex play with teens of the same sex. They touch each other's sex parts in a sexual way. This does not mean the teens are gay.

A teen may get excited seeing other teens of the same sex in the shower. This does not mean the teen is gay.

Gay teens don't choose to be gay. They have no control over this.

When a person first says, "I'm gay," or "I'm a lesbian," this is called "coming out."

Parents of gay children may feel anger, guilt, or shame. They wonder what they did wrong. It is not a parent's fault if a teen is gay. Parents should not blame themselves. There are support groups for parents of gay children.

Gay teens are often teased by other teens. Some parents reject a gay teen. Gay teens often have trouble in school. They feel alone. They may drink alcohol or take drugs to try to feel better.

Gay teens are at risk for suicide, because they feel alone and different. They are also at risk for violence called gay-bashing.

What can I do?

Teach your teen to be kind to gay people. Tell your teen being gay is not a disease. Talk to your teen about famous gay people like Ellen DeGeneres and Neil Patrick Harris.

Don't panic if your teen tells you about sex play with a teen of the same sex. This does not mean your teen is gay. Your teen may just be trying new things.

Don't blame yourself if your teen is gay. You didn't do anything wrong. Don't be angry if you find out your teen is gay. Stay calm. Your teen needs your love and support.

Don't try to talk your teen out of being gay. Don't tell your teen these feelings will go away.

Don't put down or tease your teen. Help your teen find friends who offer support. Join a support group for parents of gay children. Talking with other parents will help you give your teen love and support.

When should I get help?

- Your teen is confused about feelings for teens of the same sex.

- You have trouble accepting that your teen is gay.

You can call the Gay Lesbian Bisexual Transgender (GLBT) National Hotline at 1-888-843-4564.

Your teen can call the Trevor Project GLBT Lifeline at 1-866-488-7386 or the Gay Lesbian Bisexual Transgender National Youth Talkline at 1-800-246-7743.

Teen Safety

Notes

_____

_____

_____

_____

_____

_____

_____

_____

_____

_____

_____

_____

_____

_____

Driving

What is it?

Teen gets a driver's license and
drives a car or motorcycle. In
most states, teens can get a
driver's license at age 16.
In some states, the age is 18.

Did you know?

Most teens want to drive. It gives them freedom. It makes
them feel grown up.

Car crashes are the number 1 killer of teens in the U.S.
Some teens don't wear seatbelts. Some teens take risks
when they drive. Teens don't see risks on the road like
longtime drivers do. Teens may be looking around instead
of watching the road. This can lead to crashes.

Drunk driving can kill. No one should drive after drinking
alcohol or taking drugs. No one should ride in a car if the
driver has been drinking or taking drugs. In many states,
teens lose their license for drinking and driving. This
happens the first time a teen is caught.

Insurance rates are much higher for teens. Most insurance
companies give discounts to teens who have good grades
in school. Many high schools offer driving classes. This is a
good way for teens to learn how to drive. Teens need a lot
of practice.

Sometimes teens drive with too many people in the car. This is not safe. Driving alone is safer than with a group of friends. Friends can take a teen's mind off the road. Loud music in the car can take a teen's mind off the road.

Driving in bad weather or at night is harder. Teens need to know what to do if an accident happens.

What can I do?

Help your teen learn to drive. Let your teen drive with you in the car. Make sure your teen is a safe driver. Get your teen to take driving lessons.

Set driving rules for your teen. Here are some rules:

- Never drink and drive. Never take drugs and drive. Never ride in a car if the driver drank alcohol or took drugs.

- Never take your hands off the wheel while driving. Pull into a safe parking area to use your phone. Park when you want to send text messages, make phone calls, operate a GPS or MP3 player, or eat.

- Don't ride in a car if the driver is texting or talking on the phone. (If the driver is talking "hands-free," it may be OK. But don't ride if you don't feel safe.)

- Always wear a seat belt, even in the back seat. Never take more people in the car than there are seat belts. Everyone in the car must wear a seat belt.

- Always take money with you to call home or take a bus.
- Never let another person drive your car.
- Drive on main streets. Stay off back roads.
- Don't drive when you are tired. If you are sleepy, pull over and call home.
- Don't pick up anyone you don't know.
- Find your keys before you walk to the car. Get in the car right away, and lock all the doors.
- Never take a ride from a stranger if your car breaks down.
- Set a time for your teen to be home. Have your teen call home when running late.

Shop around for car insurance to get the best price. Decide who pays for insurance, gas, tickets, and repairs. If your teen buys an old car, help fix it up. Make sure it is safe. Teach your teen what to do if the car gets a flat tire.

If your teen is in a car crash, tell your teen to do these things:

- Call 911 if anyone is hurt.
- Call the police. Stay with the car until the police come.
- Get this information about the other driver:
  - Name
  - Phone number
  - Address
  - License plate number

- Driver's license number
- Insurance company

Your teen should also:

- Get the name and phone number of everyone who saw the crash.
- Save names, numbers, and anything else from the crash.
- Write down everything about the crash.
- Take pictures of the damage to your car and the other car if your phone has a camera.
- Report the crash to your insurance company. Do this even if it is not your fault.
- Get a copy of the police report.
- Always tell your parents.

Keep a flashlight and first-aid kit in the car. You may want your teen to have a cell phone in the car to call for help.

If your teen drinks and drives, take away your teen's license. If your teen gets a speeding ticket or comes home too late, don't let your teen drive for a month.

Go over these things with your teen before you let your teen drive alone:

- The dangers of drinking and driving
- What to do if your teen drinks alcohol and has the car
- What to do in a car crash

- Driving in bad weather or at night
- What to do if the car breaks down
- What will happen if your teen breaks one of your rules

Always know **where** your teen is going and **when** your teen will be back.

When should I get help?

- Your teen had a crash and did not report it.
- Your teen is drinking or taking drugs and driving.
- Your teen keeps getting tickets.
- Your teen does not listen to you but needs to drive because of work or school.

Alcohol

What is it?

Alcohol is something people drink that can make them high and act silly, or mean and aggressive. This is called being drunk or intoxicated. Alcohol is sometimes called booze. Beer, wine, and hard liquor are all alcohol drinks.

Did you know?

Many parents don't know the dangers of alcohol. They think drinking alcohol is not as bad as taking drugs. By age 13, 1 in 4 teens drinks alcohol. Drinking may be a sign that a teen has other problems. Teens with low self-esteem may drink alcohol to feel better.

Drinking is bad for a teen's brain. It can harm a teen's ability to think and learn.

The leading cause of teen deaths is car crashes where one driver was drunk. No one should drink and drive.

It is never too early to tell kids why drinking is bad. Some kids start to drink alcohol as young as 9. A teen can become an alcoholic. This can happen without the parents knowing it.

Teens who drink are more likely to do these things:

- Do poorly in school
- Drop out of school
- Have sex at an earlier age
- Have sex without a condom

A teen is at higher risk of drinking if these things happen:

- The teen's friends drink.
- The teen has low self-esteem.
- The teen's parents or older brothers or sisters drink.
- There is stress in the home from divorce, illness, or death.

Some teens drink 5 or more drinks at a time. This is called binge (binj) drinking. Some teens die from binge drinking.

Some drinks have more alcohol than others. Some fruit-flavored wines have 20% alcohol. The wine tastes sweet. Teens may not know the drink has so much alcohol. A teen can get drunk after one drink. This can happen with wine, beer, or other alcohol.

Some teens drink alcohol that is in the home. They often add water to the bottle to replace what they drank. Your teen needs to learn how to use alcohol safely. Teens watch how their parents use alcohol. They copy you.

Teens may drink things that have alcohol in them to get high. Some things they may drink:

- Mouthwash
- Rubbing alcohol
- Cough syrup
- Hand sanitizer

A person who sells or gives alcohol to someone under the drinking age is breaking the law. That person can go to jail. The legal age for drinking is 21. If you give alcohol to a person who is younger and something bad happens, it is your fault.

Some teens drink after school if they are alone and bored. Many teens drink to be cool or to fit in. Alcohol helps a teen feel less shy. Some teens drink when they are upset. There are groups such as AA (Alcoholics Anonymous) that help teens stop using alcohol. Some teens need to go to a hospital to stop drinking alcohol.

What can I do?

Talk with your teen about the bad things that can come from drinking alcohol. Tell your teen that people die from binge drinking. Tell your teen nobody needs to drink alcohol to fit in. Teach your teen that alcohol is bad for the growing brain. It can cause harm for life.

Teach your teen safe rules about alcohol:

- Alcohol is bad for teens.
- Never drive after drinking alcohol.
- Never let anyone drive after drinking.
- Don't drink when you are alone.
- Never drink to get drunk.
- Don't drink to feel better. Drinking does not fix problems.
- Don't drink if you are depressed or angry.

Teach your teen to decide who will drive when going out with friends. This person must not drink any alcohol. This person is called the designated driver.

Teach your teen never to get into a car if the driver drank alcohol. Make sure your teen knows to call you for a ride. Always be ready to go get your teen. Tell your teen to bring money when going out. Your teen can call home or take a bus or taxi if there is a problem.

You can make a plan with your teen. If your teen has been drinking, agree on a code word your teen can text you that means he or she has been drinking and needs a ride home. Agree that you won't talk about it when you pick up your teen that night.

Don't fight with a drunken teen. Don't let your teen go to sleep drunk. Your teen can slip into a coma and die. Walk with your teen until the alcohol gets out of the body.

Help your teen find things to do after school. Try to be there when your teen comes home from school. Know what your teen is doing after school.

Watch for signs that your teen is drinking. Here are some signs:
- Acting silly or some other strange way
- Mood swings
- Change in friends
- Telling lies
- Breath smells of alcohol
- Alcohol is missing from the home
- Missing school/grades drop

Get your teen into a group like AA if you think your teen has a problem with alcohol.

When should I get help?
- You think your teen is drinking.
- Call 911 if your teen is hard to wake up after drinking.

Drugs

What is it?

Something a person eats, smokes, sniffs, or takes in a shot with a needle to feel good or get high.

Did you know?

Drugs are everywhere. Kids as young as 8 or 9 use drugs. It is never too early to start talking with kids about why drugs are bad. A teen can die from using drugs just one time.

Teens start using drugs for many reasons:
- They want to try something new.
- They want to fit in.
- They want to feel better about themselves.
- They want to escape problems at home or school.
- Peer pressure
- They want to lose weight.

At first teens take drugs to feel good. This is called getting high. Later they need drugs to stop feeling bad. This is called drug addiction.

Some teens take prescription drugs to help them stay up late and study. Teens can get addicted to these drugs. Teens can become addicted in a short time. Parents often don't know when a teen is taking drugs.

Drugs

Here are some signs that a teen may be using drugs:

- Teen gets poor grades in school.
- Money and other things are missing from the home.
- Teen is alone most of the time.
- Teen can't get up in the morning.
- You find drugs in your teen's room.
- Teen is spending money very fast.
- Teen skips classes or doesn't go to school.
- Teen lies and steals.

Also watch for these signs:

- Changes in eating or sleeping habits
- Big change in mood
- Lack of interest in things teen used to like to do
- Fighting with friends and family
- Violent moments
- Glassy eyes
- Slurred speech
- Getting sick a lot
- Smells of drugs like pot (marijuana)

Parents may be too busy to see the signs. They may think it can't happen to their teen. Drug use can happen to anyone.

Drugs are bad for the brain. They can harm for life how a person thinks and acts.

There are many drugs. Here are the most common ones:

Marijuana Other names for marijuana are pot, weed, grass, joint, and roach. It is the most common drug. It is usually smoked but can be eaten or added to foods (brownies).

Cocaine Other names are coke, snow, and flake. It is snorted into the nose.

Crack cocaine Other names are crack, freebase rocks, and rock cocaine. This drug is smoked.

LSD This drug is also called acid. It is taken by mouth.

PCP Other names are angel dust, wack, and loveboat. It is taken by mouth.

Ecstasy Made in homemade labs. Other names are E, X, and Scooby Snacks. It can be a pill or powder. Usually taken at parties. Used by teens to get a "high" or feel good.

Speed Other names are amphetamines, black beauties, and hearts. There are many types of speed. It can be taken by mouth, smoked, snorted, or injected.

Heroin Other names are smack and horse. It is injected into a vein, snorted up the nose, or smoked.

Methamphetamine Other names are ice, crank, meth, and crystal. It comes in a crystal or powder form. It is taken by mouth.

Inhalants These are things that teens breathe in (sniff) to get high. Sniffing fumes is called huffing. Some things teens sniff are glue, gasoline, and spray cans like those from paint, cleaning products, and whipped cream.

Rohypnol (Roe-hip-nawl) Other names are roofies, roach, forget-me pill and date rape. It is slipped into drinks at parties. It causes a person to pass out or have sudden feelings of being drunk.

Prescription drugs A drug prescribed by a doctor for one person that is then used by another person. It is used to get high, treat pain, or because a teen thinks it will help with studying.

What can I do?

Start talking with your teen early about why drugs are bad. Talk about all the bad things that can happen when taking drugs. Teach your teen to say "no" to drugs. Say this over and over again. Make it clear to your teen that drugs are bad.

Tell your teen that some people put drugs in other people's drinks. Your teen should never leave a drink and come back to drink it.

Teens who take drugs often have other problems. Listen to what your teen says to you. Help your teen. If you don't know what to do, get outside help. Watch for signs that your teen may be taking drugs. (See page 159.) Tell your teen not to take any drugs to help with studying. It can lead to addiction or being "hooked."

Watch for signs that your teen may be huffing. Some things to look for are:

- Sores or rash near nose and mouth
- Paint on face or clothes

- Smell of chemicals on clothes or in teen's room
- Red eyes
- Runny nose
- Unsteady walk

Here are some other things you can do:

- Help your teen find things to do after school. Know what your teen does after school.
- Ask your teen what goes on away from home. Check to see if it's true.
- Don't leave your teen alone a lot.
- Get to know your teen's friends and the teen's parents. Help your teen pick good friends.
- Get your teen into sports or other good groups like Boys and Girls Clubs.

If you find drugs in your teen's room, do something right away. Your teen can die from taking drugs. Talk to your teen about what you found. Get outside help right away.

Talk honestly with your teen if other members of the family have a problem with drugs. Talk about addiction. Talk about how hard it is to stop taking drugs. Talk about how drugs ruin people's lives.

When should I get help?

Get help right away if you think your teen is taking drugs. See the list of places to call on page 4.

Smoking

What is it?

It is breathing smoke from a cigarette into the lungs. It is a bad habit. It costs a lot of money. It makes people sick. People die from smoking.

Did you know?

Children as young as 8 try smoking. About 1 in 3 teens who try smoking becomes a steady smoker. Smoking is like a drug. Once you start, it is very hard to stop.

Some kids chew tobacco called "snuff." This is just as bad as smoking. It can cause mouth and throat cancer. It can also cause tooth loss and gum disease.

Teens smoke for many reasons:
- They want to look cool. They want to look or feel grown-up.
- Someone smokes at home.
- Their friends smoke.
- They are bored. They want to know what it's like to smoke.
- They are hungry or want to lose weight.
- They feel stress at home or school.
- They see people smoke in the movies and on TV.

What can I do?

Start talking with your teen early about why smoking is bad.

Here are some things you can tell your teen about smoking:

- Once you start smoking, it's very hard to stop.
- Smoking costs a lot of money. You can save a lot of money by not smoking.
- It gives you bad breath and makes your teeth yellow.
- No one wants to kiss a smoker.
- Smoking causes cancer. It makes your heart and lungs sick.
- Smoking makes you do poorly in sports. It makes it harder for you to breathe.
- You may get kicked out of school if you are caught smoking.

Teens need to learn to like themselves. You can help. Tell your teen nobody needs to smoke to fit in or look cool. Teens learn by example. If you smoke, your teen will also smoke. This may be a good time for you to stop smoking. Get your family to help you stop. Let your teen see how hard it is to stop.

Get your teen into sports, band, or other things that don't allow smoking. Encourage your teen to have friends who don't smoke. Help your teen plan how to say "no" when friends suggest smoking. Here are some things to say:

- "No thanks, I like myself too much to smoke."

- "Smoking will hurt my health."
- "My coach will kick me off the team if he catches me smoking."
- "I will be grounded for a month if my parents catch me."
- "My parents will not let me use the car if I smoke."

Look for signs that your teen smokes:

- Cigarette butts in pockets
- Yellow fingers
- Hair and clothes smell of smoke

Do these things if your teen smokes:

- Talk with your teen's teacher about a school project on why smoking is bad. Talk about what happens to your body when you smoke. This might help your teen decide to quit.
- Promise to buy your teen something after a month of no smoking.
- Call the American Lung Association at 1-800-586-4872. They can help you find help for your teen.
- Ask your teen's school about a program to help your teen stop smoking.
- Talk with your teen's coach or counselor about other things to try.

When should I get help?

Get help if your teen smokes, or if you think your teen is smoking. See the list of places to call on page 4.

Body Piercing

What is it?

Body piercing is making holes in the skin for rings or studs.

Did you know?

Many teens have their body pierced. Common places are the face, ears, eyebrow, belly button, and tongue. Teens get pierced because they think it looks good. They want people to see them and talk about it.

Some teens get too many piercings. This can be a sign of other problems. Teens can get infection, hepatitis B or hepatitis C, and tetanus from body piercing. These are very serious diseases.

Some teens use a sewing needle from home to make a hole in the skin. This can cause infection. Here are some signs of infection:

- Redness around the hole
- Red streaks on the skin
- Yellow liquid (pus) oozing from hole
- Swelling
- Pain

Some states have laws for body piercing. Some places use a machine called a piercing gun. It is hard to clean.

It is safe only for piercing the earlobe. People can get disease and infection from the tool or needle used for piercing. New needles or clean (sterile) tools must be used each time. New latex gloves need to be worn each time.

No one should get a piercing while high on drugs or alcohol. They may not know what they are doing. Belly-button piercing takes up to a year to heal. A teen can get a very bad infection.

What can I do?

Tell your teen that piercing can make a person sick. Have your teen wait 2 months before getting a piercing. Tell your teen to take time to think about it.

If your teen is sure about getting pierced, help your teen pick a safe place to have it done. Make sure your teen has shots for hepatitis and tetanus.

Don't get upset if your teen gets pierced. Help your teen stop at one piercing.

When should I get help?

- Your teen insists on getting body piercing. Find a safe place for your teen.
- Your teen has signs of infection like redness, pus, heat, and pain.
- Your teen has more than 2 body piercings.

Tattoos

What is it?

Tattoos are marks or designs in the skin that don't come off. They are made by injecting ink under the skin with needles. Tattoos stay on the skin forever.

Did you know?

Many people get tattoos. It does not mean they are bad or in gangs.

It is very hard to get rid of a tattoo. It costs a lot of money. Some of the tattoo may not come off. Some teens pick a design that is not right for an adult. A teen will be stuck with the tattoo for life. Many adults wish they did not get a tattoo when they were a teen.

A person can get infections, hepatitis B or C, and other diseases from getting a tattoo. People high on drugs or alcohol should not get a tattoo. They may not know what they are doing.

Some states have laws for safe tattoos. People should only go to legal tattoo places. In many states, teens under 18 need a parent's consent to get tattoos. Many teens sign their mom's or dad's name. They are breaking the law.

What can I do?

If your teen wants a tattoo, make sure your teen knows that tattoos don't come off easily. Have your teen ask a doctor how hard it is to take off a tattoo. Talk to your teen about other ways to look cool, like hair color and style.

Learn about the laws in your state. Make sure your teen knows the law. Ask your teen to wait 1 or 2 months before getting a tattoo. Your teen should think it over. A tattoo is forever. Will your teen want it in 10 years? Have your teen talk to people who wish they did not get a tattoo.

If your teen is sure about getting a tattoo, help pick a good design. Have the tattoo put where it can be covered with clothes. Have the tattoo done at a safe and legal place.

Make sure your teen has shots for hepatitis and tetanus.

If your teen gets a tattoo, don't get upset. Help your teen to stop at one tattoo.

When should I get help?

- Your teen wants a tattoo. You want to find a safe and legal place.
- Your teen got a tattoo. The skin shows signs of infection like redness, pus, and heat.

Gangs

What is it?

A gang is a group of people who have rules and a leader. They hang out together. They try to look the same. They wear the same kinds of clothes.

Did you know?

Gangs are everywhere. More boys than girls are in gangs. Most teens in gangs are between the ages of 12 and 17. Many gangs use drugs, steal, and break laws. They tag (use spray paint to write messages on walls), sell drugs, and commit crimes. Sometimes they use guns. Many teens die or get badly hurt in gangs.

Here are some reasons teens join gangs:

- They want to fit in.
- They want love and support.
- They think it's cool to be in a gang.
- They want to feel a part of something.
- They want to make money.
- They want respect.
- They want power by controlling their neighborhood.
- They are scared if they don't join, or they feel they have no choice.

Teens who get lots of love and support from their family may not feel the need to join a gang. They don't need gangs for love and support.

What can I do?

Find out what your teen thinks about gangs. Talk with your teen about the dangers of being in a gang.

Ask yourself if you spend enough time with your teen. Many teens are alone too much. They get into gangs because they have nothing to do. Spend time together as a family. Start a family project. Do a sport as a family.

Watch for these signs that your teen may be in a gang:

- Starts wearing gang clothing, like baggy pants, bandannas, etc.
- You find gang writing on school books or other things.
- Teen starts hanging out with gang-type friends.

Teens need other teens. Help your teen find safe clubs to join. Some good places to find groups:

- YMCA
- Church or other place of worship
- School
- Community centers

Talk to the school or police about gangs in your area. Find out what you can do. Watch how your teen dresses. Don't let your teen wear gang colors. Your teen can get hurt or killed.

When should I get help?

- Your teen is in a gang.
- You are worried your teen will join a gang.
- Your teen is bullied by a gang.
- Your teen feels pressure to join a gang.

Word List

A

- **abortion**—An operation done by a doctor to end a pregnancy.
- **abstinence**—Not having sex.
- **abuse**—To hurt or harm by what you do to yourself or other people.
- **acne**—Pimples or red rash on the face that comes with hormone changes.
- **addiction**—A strong need or desire to do something like smoke or take drugs.
- **adoption**—To give a child to another family, or take a child into your family.
- **alcoholic**—A person who cannot control how much alcohol he or she drinks.
- **Alcoholics Anonymous (AA)**—A group that helps people stop drinking alcohol.
- **allowance**—Money given to teens on a regular basis.
- **anal sex**—Putting the penis into the anus.
- **anus**—External opening of the rectum.
- **appetite**—A normal desire for food.

B

- **binge eating**—Eating large amounts of food in a short time.

- **birth control**—Things people use to not get pregnant when they have sex.
- **BM**—bowel movement.
- **booze**—A slang word for drinks that have alcohol.
- **Boys and Girls Club**—A place to go in the neighborhood that has activities for teens.
- **breast**—Part of the chest. In women, breast glands make milk after childbirth.
- **bully**—Someone who picks on people to have power over them.

C

- **cervix**—The opening of the uterus into the vagina.
- **cigarette**—Tobacco rolled in paper for smoking. People who smoke can get addicted. Smoking causes cancer and many other diseases.
- **circumcision**—An operation to remove the foreskin around the penis.
- **chores**—Things that people must do around the house.
- **coitus**— Another word for sex.
- **coma**—A deep sleep-like state caused by sickness or injury.
- **condom**—A latex cover put on a hard penis before sex. It helps prevent pregnancy and many sexually transmitted diseases.
- **contraception**—Another word for birth control.
- **copulation**—Another word for sex.
- **curfew**—The time a person needs to be home.

- **cutting**—Using something sharp to cut through the skin as a way to get rid of feeling tense.
- **cyberbullying**—Using the Internet to bully.

D

- **deodorant**—A spray, cream, or other thing put on the body to stop bad body smell.
- **designated driver**—A person who does not drink alcohol in order to safely drive other people home.
- **drinking**—A word used to mean drinking liquids that have alcohol.

E

- **ejaculate**—When semen comes out of the penis during orgasm.
- **electronic device**—Camera, cell phone, electronic tablet, iPod, laptop.
- **erection**—A hard penis.

F

- **foreskin**—Loose skin around the tip of the penis. It can be removed by an operation called circumcision.

G

- **gay**—Having a strong attraction to people of the same sex; homosexual.
- **gay bashing**—Making fun of or hurting someone because that person is gay.
- **genitals**—Parts of the body used in sex.

- **grounding**—A type of punishment that does not allow a teen to go out with friends for a period of time.

H

- **hormonal implant**—A very thin tube placed under the skin to prevent pregnancy.
- **hormones**—Chemicals made in the body to do certain things.
- **huffing**—Breathing or sniffing fumes from glue or spray cans to get high.

I

- **infection**—Sickness caused by germs you cannot see. An infection can happen inside the body or on the skin. Signs of skin infection are redness, heat, pain, and liquid or pus oozing from the skin.
- **intoxicated**—Another word for being drunk.
- **IUD**—Intrauterine device. A small T-shaped piece of plastic put in the uterus to prevent pregnancy.

L

- **laxative**—Medicine you take to help you have a BM (bowel movement).
- **learning disorder**—Trouble reading and learning.
- **lesbian**—A girl who is attracted to other girls.
- **library**—A place where books are kept. People go to the library to read books or to take books home for a period of time.

M

- **MyPlate**—a picture of a dinner plate that shows how much food to eat from each food group for each meal.

O

- **oral sex**—Putting the mouth on the penis or the vagina.
- **orgasm**—Another word for climax or coming.
- **ovulation**—When an egg comes out of a woman's ovary.

P

- **peer pressure**—When friends try to get a person to do something.
- **period**—The bloody discharge that comes out of a girl's vagina each month. This is called menstruation.
- **prenatal**—The time before childbirth when a woman is expecting a baby.
- **puberty**—The time of fast growth when boys' and girls' bodies change from a child to an adult.
- **punishment**—A penalty given to a person for doing something wrong.
- **pus**—A thick liquid that comes out of the body when there is an infection. The liquid is usually yellow or green and can smell bad.

R

- **rape**—Forcing someone to have sex.

S

- **scrotum**—The pouch or sac on the outside of a man's body behind the penis that holds the testicles (balls).

Word List

- **semen**—Thick white fluid that comes out of the penis during ejaculation.
- **sexting**—Sending sex photos or words with an electronic device like a cell phone.
- **sperm**—The man's seed. Sperm combines with the woman's egg to make a baby.
- **spermicide**—A cream or foam that kills sperm.
- **steroid**—Drugs taken by people to get stronger and do better in sports. Steroids are sometimes ordered by doctors for certain diseases.

T

- **teen years**—In this book, the teen years refer to ages 9–19 years.
- **testicles**—The part of the man's body that makes sperm. Also called balls.
- **transgender**—A person who feels he or she was born in the wrong body. The person may have the body of a male but feel and think like a female. The person dresses and acts like a female. Or it can be a person with a female body who feels like a male and dresses and acts like one.
- **tutors**—Special teachers to help people with school work or to learn certain things.

V

- **violence**—The use of force or power to hurt, harm, damage, destroy, abuse, or kill.

W

- **wet dream**—Ejaculation during sleep.

What's in This Book
From A to Z

People We Want to Thank

We want to thank the following people for their help with this book:

Helen Acevez

Albert Barnett, MD

Art Brown, BA, MA

Diane Brown, MPH

Frank J. Brown, BS, MBA

Angela Casares

Angelique Maree Crain, AB, MA

Lourdes Cruz

Robert Cummings, MD, Ph.D.

Maricela Estrada

Gene Getz Jr.

Michelle Getz

JoAnn Heller

Patty Herrera

Cpl. Scott Irwin

Shanine Jackson

Hannah Lee

Judi Leonard, MSN, PNP, CS

Thomas R. Mayer, MD, MBA

Nancy L. McDade

Kimberly Miller, JD, MA, LAMFT

Mona Moreno

Richard C. Palmer, MD

Greg Perez, BS

Kemy Pyper

Ruby Raya-Morones, MD

Gary Richwald, MD, MPH

Steven Rosenberg, MD

Cpl. Victor Rubalcava

Nancy Rushton, RN, BSN

Michael Satin

Andrew Scott, BA, B.Ed

Emily Scott, B.Ed

Jennifer Ann Scott

Jane Song

Benz Teeranitayatarn

Dylann Tharp

Irene Verdi

Camille Wall, MSW, LCSW

Vivian Wilson

The What To Do For Health Book Series
All books available in English and Spanish.

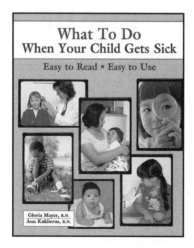

ISBN 978-0-9701245-0-0
$12.95

What To Do When Your Child Gets Sick*

There are many things you can do at home for your child. At last, an easy-to-read, easy-to-use book written by 2 nurses who know. This book tells you:

- What to look for when your child is sick.
- When to call the doctor.
- How to take your child's temperature.
- What to do when your child has the flu.
- How to care for cuts and scrapes.
- What to feed your child when he or she is sick.
- How to stop the spread of infection.
- How to prevent accidents around your home.
- What to do in an emergency.

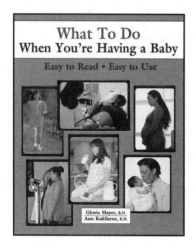

ISBN 978-0-9701245-6-2
$12.95

What To Do When You're Having a Baby

There are many things a woman can do to have a healthy baby. Here's an easy-to-read, easy-to-use book written by two nurses that tells you:

- How to get ready for pregnancy.
- About the health care you need during pregnancy.
- Things you should not do when you are pregnant.
- How to take care of yourself so you have a healthy baby.
- Body changes you have each month.
- Simple things you can do to feel better.
- Warning signs of problems and what to do about them.
- All about labor and delivery.
- How to feed and care for your new baby.

*Also available in Vietnamese, Chinese, and Korean.
To order or for more information, please email books@iha4health.org or call 1-800-434-4633.

The What To Do For Health Book Series
All books available in English and Spanish.

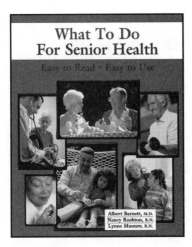

ISBN 978-0-9701245-4-8
$12.95

What To Do For Senior Health*

There are many things that you can do to take charge of your health during your senior years. This book tells about:

- Body changes that come with aging.
- Common health problems of seniors.
- Things to consider about health insurance.
- How to choose a doctor and where to get health care.
- Buying and taking medicines.
- Simple things you can do to prevent falls and accidents.
- What you can do to stay healthy.

ISBN 978-0-9720148-0-9
$12.95

What To Do For Healthy Teeth

It is important to take good care of your teeth from an early age. This book tells how to do that. It also explains all about teeth, gums, and how dentists work with you to keep your teeth healthy.

- How to care for your teeth and gums.
- What you need to care for your teeth and gums.
- Caring for your teeth when you're having a baby.
- Caring for your child's teeth.
- When to call the dentist.
- What to expect at a dental visit.
- Dental care needs for seniors.
- What to do if you hurt your mouth or teeth.

*Also available in Vietnamese.
To order or for more information, please email books@iha4health.org or call 1-800-434-4633.

The What To Do For Health Book Series
All books available in English and Spanish.

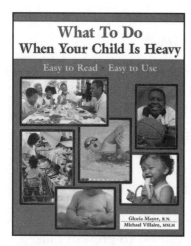

ISBN 978-0-9721048-4-7
$12.95

What To Do
When Your Child Is Heavy

There are many things you can do to help your heavy child live a healthy lifestyle. Here's an easy-to-read, easy-to-use book that tells you:

- How to tell if your child is heavy.
- How to shop and pay for healthy food.
- Dealing with your heavy child's feelings and self-esteem.
- How to read the Nutrition Facts Label.
- Healthy breakfasts, lunches, and dinners.
- Correct portion sizes.
- Why exercise is so important.
- Tips for eating healthy when you eat out.
- Information on diabetes and other health problems of heavy children.

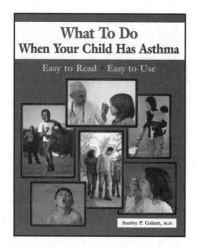

ISBN 978-0-9720148-6-1
$12.95

What To Do
When Your Child Has Asthma

Having a child with asthma can be scary. This easy-to-read, easy-to-use book tells you what you can do to help your child deal with asthma:

- How to tell if your child needs help right away.
- Signs that your child has asthma.
- Triggers for an asthma attack.
- Putting together an Asthma Action Plan.
- How to use a peak flow meter.
- The different kinds of asthma medicine.
- How to talk to your child's day care and teachers about your child's asthma.
- Making sure your child gets enough exercise.
- Helping your child to take his or her asthma medicine the right way.
- What to do for problems like upset stomach, hay fever, and stuffy nose.

To order or for more information, please email books@iha4health.org or call 1-800-434-4633.